JOHN MARSHALL
AND THE CONSTITUTION

EXTRA-ILLUSTRATED EDITION

∵

VOLUME 16
THE CHRONICLES
OF AMERICA SERIES
ALLEN JOHNSON
EDITOR

GERHARD R. LOMER
CHARLES W. JEFFERYS
ASSISTANT EDITORS

Gravure, Anderson-Lamb Co. N.Y.

JOHN MARSHALL
AND THE CONSTITUTION

A CHRONICLE OF
THE SUPREME COURT
BY EDWARD S. CORWIN

NEW HAVEN: YALE UNIVERSITY PRESS
TORONTO: GLASGOW, BROOK & CO.
LONDON: HUMPHREY MILFORD
OXFORD UNIVERSITY PRESS

E
173
C56
Vol. 16

13858

CONTENTS

I. THE ESTABLISHMENT OF THE NATIONAL
JUDICIARY   Page 1

II. MARSHALL'S EARLY YEARS   " 25

III. JEFFERSON'S WAR ON THE JUDICIARY   " 53

IV. THE TRIAL OF AARON BURR   " 86

V. THE TENETS OF NATIONALISM   " 121

VI. THE SANCTITY OF CONTRACTS   " 147

VII. THE MENACE OF STATE RIGHTS   " 173

VIII. AMONG FRIENDS AND NEIGHBORS   " 198

IX. EPILOGUE   " 224

BIBLIOGRAPHICAL NOTE   " 233

INDEX   " 237

ILLUSTRATIONS

JOHN MARSHALL

Engraving by A. B. Durand, after a painting by
H. Inman. Published in *The National Portrait
Gallery of Distinguished Americans.* *Frontispiece*

OLIVER ELLSWORTH

Engraving by E. McKenzie, after a painting by
J. Herring. Published in *The National Portrait
Gallery of Distinguished Americans.* *Facing page* *20*

JOHN MARSHALL'S HOUSE IN RICHMOND

Photograph by H. P. Cook, Richmond, Virginia. " " *36*

JOSEPH STORY

Engraving, after a crayon drawing by his son,
William Wetmore Story, the poet and sculptor. " " *116*

ROBERT R. LIVINGSTON

Engraving by E. McKenzie, after a painting by
John Vanderlyn. " " *132*

JAMES KENT

Painting by Rembrandt Peale. In the office of
the Corporation Counsel, City Hall, New York.
Owned by the Corporation. Reproduced by
courtesy of the Municipal Art Commission of the
City of New York. " " *164*

JOHN McLEAN

Painting by Thomas Sully. In the Pennsylvania
Academy of the Fine Arts, Philadelphia. " " *228*

JOHN MARSHALL AND THE CONSTITUTION

∵

CHAPTER I

THE ESTABLISHMENT OF THE NATIONAL JUDICIARY

THE monarch of ancient times mingled the functions of priest and judge. It is therefore not altogether surprising that even today a judicial system should be stamped with a certain resemblance to an ecclesiastical hierarchy. If the Church of the Middle Ages was "an army encamped on the soil of Christendom, with its outposts everywhere, subject to the most efficient discipline, animated with a common purpose, every soldier panoplied with inviolability and armed with the tremendous weapons which slew the soul," the same words, slightly varied, may be applied to the Federal Judiciary created by the American Constitution. The Judiciary of the United States, though numerically not a large body, reaches through its process every part of the nation; its ascendancy is primarily a moral one; it is kept in conformity with final authority by the machinery of appeal; it is "animated with a common purpose"; its members are "panoplied" with what is practically a life tenure of their posts; and it is "armed with the tremendous weapons" which slay legislation. And if the voice of the Church was the voice of God, so the voice of the Court is the voice of the American people as this is recorded in the Constitution.

The Hildebrand of American constitutionalism is John Marshall. The contest carried on by the greatest of the Chief Justices for the principles to-day associated with his name is very like that waged by the greatest of the Popes for the supremacy of the Papacy. Both fought with intellectual weapons. Both addressed their appeal to the minds and hearts of men. Both died before the triumph of their respective causes and amid circumstances of great discouragement. Both worked through and for great institutions which preceded them and which have survived them. And, as the achievements of Hildebrand cannot be justly appreciated without some knowledge of the ecclesiastical system which he did so much to develop, neither can the career of John

Marshall be understood without some knowledge of the organization of the tribunal through which he wrought and whose power he did so much to exalt. The first chapter in the history of John Marshall and his influence upon the laws of the land must therefore inevitably deal with the historical conditions underlying the judicial system of which it is the capstone.

The vital defect of the system of government provided by the soon obsolete Articles of Confederation lay in the fact that it operated not upon the individual citizens of the United States but upon the States in their corporate capacities. As a consequence the prescribed duties of any law passed by Congress in pursuance of powers derived from the Articles of Confederation could not be enforced. Theoretically, perhaps, Congress had the right to coerce the States to perform their duties; at any rate, a Congressional Committee headed by Madison so decided at the very moment (1781) when the Articles were going into effect. But practically such a course of coercion, requiring in the end the exercise of military power, was out of the question. Whence were to come the forces for military operations against recalcitrant States? From sister States which had themselves neglected their constitutional duties on various occasions? The history of the German Empire has demonstrated that the principle of state coercion is entirely feasible when a single powerful State dominates the rest of the confederation. But the Confederation of 1781 possessed no such giant member; it approximated a union of equals, and in theory it was entirely such.[1]

In the Federal Convention of 1787 the idea of state coercion required little discussion; for the

[1] By the Articles of Confederation Congress itself was made "the last resort of all disputes and differences . . . between two or more States concerning boundary, jurisdiction, or any other cause whatever." It was also authorized to appoint "courts for the trial of piracies and felonies committed on the high seas" and "for receiving and determining finally appeals in all cases of capture." But even before the Articles had gone into operation, Congress had, as early as 1779, established a tribunal for such appeals, the old Court of Appeals in Cases of Capture. Thus at the very outset, and at a time when the doctrine of state sovereignty was dominant, the practice of appeals from state courts to a supreme national tribunal was employed, albeit within a restricted sphere. Yet it is less easy to admit that the Court of Appeals was, as has been contended by one distinguished authority, "not simply the predecessor but one of the origins of the Supreme Court of the United States." The Supreme Court is the creation of the Constitution itself; it is the final interpreter of the law in every field of national power; and its decrees are carried into effect by the force and authority of the Government of which it is one of the three coördinate branches. That earlier tribunal, the Court of Appeals in Cases of Capture, was, on the other hand, a purely legislative creation; its jurisdiction was confined to a single field, and that of importance only in time of war; and the enforcement of its decisions rested with the state governments.

members were soon convinced that it involved an impracticable, illogical, and unjust principle. The prevailing view was voiced by Oliver Ellsworth before the Connecticut ratifying convention: "We see how necessary for Union is a coercive principle. No man pretends to the contrary. . . . The only question is, shall it be a coercion of law or a coercion of arms? There is no other possible alternative. Where will those who oppose a coercion of law come out? . . . A necessary consequence of their principles is a war of the States one against the other. I am for coercion by law, that coercion which acts only upon delinquent individuals." If anything, these words somewhat exaggerate the immunity of the States from direct control by the National Government, for, as James Madison pointed out in the *Federalist*, "in several cases . . . they [the States] must be viewed and proceeded against in their collective capacities." Yet Ellsworth stated correctly the controlling principle of the new government: it was to operate upon individuals through laws interpreted and enforced by its own courts

A Federal Judiciary was provided for in every plan offered on the floor of the Federal Convention. There was also a fairly general agreement among the members on the question of "judicial independence." Indeed, most of the state constitutions already made the tenure of the principal judges dependent upon their good behavior, though in some cases judges were removable, as in England, upon the joint address of the two Houses of the Legislature. That the Federal judges should be similarly removable by the President upon the application of the Senate and House of Representatives was proposed late in the Convention by Dickinson of Delaware, but the suggestion received the vote of only one State. In the end it was all but unanimously agreed that the Federal judges should be removable only upon conviction following impeachment.

But, while the Convention was in accord on this matter, another question, that of the organization of the new judiciary, evoked the sharpest disagreement among its members. All believed that there must be a national Supreme Court to impress upon the national statutes a construction that should be uniformly binding throughout the country; but they disagreed upon the question whether there should be inferior national courts. Rutledge of South Carolina wanted the state courts to be used as national courts of the first instance and argued that a right of appeal to the supreme national tribunal would be quite sufficient "to secure the national rights and uniformity of judgment." But Madison pointed out that such an arrangement would cause appeals to be multiplied most oppressively and that, furthermore, it would provide no remedy for improper verdicts resulting from local prejudices. A compromise was reached by leaving the question to the discretion of Congress. The champions of local liberties, however, both at Philadelphia and in the state conventions continued to the end to urge that Congress should utilize the state courts as national tribunals of the first instance. The significance of this plea should be emphasized because the time was to come when the same interest would argue that for the Supreme Court to take appeals from the state courts on any account was a humiliation to the latter and an utter disparagement of State Rights.

Even more important than the relation of the Supreme Court to the judicial systems of the States was the question of its relation to the Constitution as a governing instrument. Though the idea that courts were entitled to pronounce on the constitutionality of legislative acts had received countenance in a few dicta in some of the States and

perhaps in one or two decisions, this idea was still
at best in 1787 but the germ of a possible institution.   It is not surprising, therefore, that no such
doctrine found place in the resolutions of the Virginia plan which came before the Convention.   By
the sixth resolution of this plan the national legislature was to have the power of negativing all
state laws which, in its opinion, contravened "the
Articles of Union, or any treaty subsisting under
the authority of the Union," and by the eighth
resolution "a convenient number of the national
judiciary" were to be associated with the Executive, "with authority to examine every act of the
national legislature before it shall operate, and
every act of a particular legislature before a negative thereon shall be final" and to impose a qualified
veto in either case.

But, as discussion in the Convention proceeded,
three principles obtained clearer and clearer recognition, if not from all its members, certainly from
the great majority of them: first, that the Constitution is law, in the sense of being enforcible by
courts; secondly, that it is supreme law, with which
ordinary legislation must be in harmony to be valid;
and thirdly — a principle deducible from the doctrine of the separation of powers — that, while the

function of making new law belongs to the legislative branch of the Government, that of expound-
ing the standing law, of which the Constitution
would be part and parcel, belongs to the Judiciary.
The final disposition of the question of insuring the
conformity of ordinary legislation to the Constitution turned to no small extent on the recognition of
these three great principles.

The proposal to endow Congress with the power
to negative state legislation having been rejected
by the Convention, Luther Martin of Maryland
moved that "the legislative acts of the United
States made in virtue and in pursuance of the
Articles of Union, and all treaties made or ratified under the authority of the United States, shall
be the supreme law of the respective States, and
the judiciaries of the several States shall be bound
thereby in their decisions, anything in the respective laws of the individual States to the contrary
notwithstanding." The motion was agreed to
without a dissenting voice and, with some slight
changes, became Article VIII of the report of the
Committee of Detail of the 7th of August, which in
turn became "the linch-pin of the Constitution."[1]
Then, on the 27th of August, it was agreed that

[1] Article VI, paragraph 2.

"the jurisdiction of the Supreme Court" should "extend to all cases arising under the laws passed by the Legislature of the United States," whether, that is, such laws should be in pursuance of the Constitution or not. The foundation was thus laid for the Supreme Court to claim the right to review any state decision challenging on constitutional grounds the validity of any act of Congress. Presently this foundation was broadened by the substitution of the phrase "judicial power of the United States" for the phrase "jurisdiction of the Supreme Court," and also by the insertion of the words "this Constitution" and "the" before the word "laws" in what ultimately became Article III of the Constitution. The implications of the phraseology of this part of the Constitution are therefore significant:

Section I. The judicial power of the United States shall be vested in one Supreme Court, and in such inferior courts as the Congress may from time to time ordain and establish. The judges, both of the Supreme and inferior courts, shall hold their offices during good behavior, and shall at stated times receive for their services a compensation which shall not be diminished during their continuance in office.

Section II. 1. The judicial power shall extend to all cases in law and equity arising under this Constitution, the laws of the United States, and treaties made, or which shall be made, under their authority; to all cases affecting ambassadors, other public ministers, and consuls; to all cases of admiralty and maritime jurisdiction; to controversies to which the United States shall be a party; to controversies between two or more States, between a State and citizens of another State, between citizens of different States, between citizens of the same State claiming lands under grants of different States, and between a State, or the citizens thereof, and foreign states, citizens, or subjects.

Such, then, is the verbal basis of the power of the courts, and particularly of the Supreme Court, to review the legislation of any State, with reference to the Constitution, to acts of Congress, or to treaties of the United States.   Nor can there be much doubt that the members of the Convention were also substantially agreed that the Supreme Court was endowed with the further right to pass upon the constitutionality of acts of Congress. The available evidence strictly contemporaneous with the framing and ratification of the Constitution shows us seventeen of the fifty-five members of the Convention asserting the existence of this prerogative in unmistakable terms and only three using language that can be construed to the contrary. More striking than that, however, is the fact that these seventeen names include fully three-fourths of the leaders of the Convention, four of the five members of the Committee of Detail which drafted the Constitution, and four of the five members of the Committee of Style which gave the Constitution its final form. And these were precisely the members who expressed themselves on all the interesting and vital subjects before the Convention, because they were its statesmen and articulate members.[1]

No part of the Constitution has realized the hopes of its framers more brilliantly than has Article III, where the judicial power of the United States is defined and organized, and no part has shown itself to be more adaptable to the developing needs of a growing nation. Nor is the reason obscure: no part came from the hands of the framers in more fragmentary shape or left more to the discretion of Congress and the Court.

Congress is thus placed under constitutional obligation to establish one Supreme Court, but the size of that Court is for Congress itself to determine, as well as whether there shall be any inferior Federal

[1] The entries under the names of these members in the Index to Max Farrand's *Records of the Federal Convention* occupy fully thirty columns, as compared with fewer than half as many columns under the names of all remaining members.

Courts at all. What, it may be asked, is the significance of the word "shall" in Section II? Is it merely permissive or is it mandatory? And, in either event, when does a case arise under the Constitution or the laws of the United States? Here, too, are questions which are left for Congress in the first instance and for the Supreme Court in the last. Further, the Supreme Court is given "original jurisdiction" in certain specified cases and "appellate jurisdiction" in all others — subject, however, to "such exceptions and under such regulations as the Congress shall make." Finally, the whole question of the relation of the national courts to the state judiciaries, though it is elaborately discussed by Alexander Hamilton in the *Federalist*, is left by the Constitution itself to the practically undirected wisdom of Congress, in the exercise of its power to pass "all laws which shall be necessary and proper for carrying into execution"[1] its own powers and those of the other departments of the Government.

Almost the first official act of the Senate of the United States, after it had perfected its own organization, was the appointment of a committee "to bring in a bill for organizing the judiciary of the United States." This committee consisted of eight

[1] Article I, section VIII, 18.

members, five of whom, including Oliver Ellsworth, its chairman, had been members of the Federal Convention. To Ellsworth is to be credited largely the authorship of the great Judiciary Act of September 24, 1789, the essential features of which still remain after 130 years in full force and effect.

This famous measure created a chief justiceship and five associate justiceships for the Supreme Court; fifteen District Courts, one for each State of the Union and for each of the two Territories, Kentucky and Ohio; and, to stand between these, three Circuit Courts consisting of two Supreme Court justices and the local district judge. The "cases" and "controversies" comprehended by the Act fall into three groups: first, those brought to enforce the national laws and treaties, original jurisdiction of which was assigned to the District Courts; secondly, controversies between citizens of different States[1]; lastly, cases brought originally under a state law and in a State Court but finally coming to involve some claim of right based on the National Constitution, laws, or treaties. For these the twenty-fifth section of the Act provided that,

[1] Where the national jurisdiction was extended to these in the interest of providing an impartial tribunal, it was given to the Circuit Courts.

where the decision of the highest State Court competent under the state law to pass upon the case was adverse to the claim thus set up, an appeal on the issue should lie to the Supreme Court. This twenty-fifth section received the hearty approval of the champions of State Rights, though later on it came to be to them an object of fiercest resentment. In the Senate, as in the Convention, the artillery of these gentlemen was trained upon the proposed inferior Federal Judiciary, which they pictured as a sort of Gargantua ready at any moment "to swallow up the state courts."

The first nominations for the Supreme Court were sent in by Washington two days after he had signed the Judiciary Act. As finally constituted, the original bench consisted of John Jay of New York as Chief Justice, and of John Rutledge of South Carolina, William Cushing of Massachusetts, John Blair of Virginia, James Wilson of Pennsylvania, and James Iredell of North Carolina as Associate Justices. All were known to be champions of the Constitution, three had been members of the Federal Convention, four had held high judicial offices in their home States, and all but Jay were on record as advocates of the principle of judicial review. Jay was one of the authors of the *Federalist,* had achieved a great diplomatic reputation in the negotiations of 1782, and possessed the political backing of the powerful Livingston family of New York.

The Judiciary Act provided for two terms of court annually, one commencing the first Monday of February, and the other on the first Monday of August. On February 2, 1790, the Court opened its doors for the first time in an upper room of the Exchange in New York City. Up to the February term of 1793 it had heard but five cases, and until the accession of Marshall it had decided but fifty-five. The justices were largely occupied in what one of them described as their "post-boy duties," that is, in riding their circuits. At first the justices rode in pairs and were assigned to particular circuits. As a result of this practice, the Southern justices were forced each year to make two trips of nearly two thousand miles each and, in order to hold court for two weeks, often passed two months on the road. In 1792, however, Congress changed the law to permit the different circuits to be taken in turn and by single justices, and in the meantime the Court had, in 1791, followed the rest of the Government to Philadelphia, a rather more central seat. Then, in 1802, the abolition of the August term eased the burdens of the justices still more.

But of course they still had to put up with bad roads, bad inns, and bad judicial quarters or sometimes none at all.

Yet that the life of a Supreme Court justice was not altogether one of discomfort is shown by the following alluring account of the travels of Justice Cushing on circuit: "He traveled over the whole of the Union, holding courts in Virginia, the Carolinas, and Georgia. His traveling equipage was a four-wheeled phaeton, drawn by a pair of horses, which he drove. It was remarkable for its many ingenious arrangements (all of his contrivance) for carrying books, choice groceries, and other comforts. Mrs. Cushing always accompanied him, and generally read aloud while riding. His faithful servant Prince, a jet-black negro, whose parents had been slaves in the family and who loved his master with unbounded affection, followed."[1] Compared with that of a modern judge always confronted with a docket of eight or nine hundred cases in arrears, Justice Cushing's lot was perhaps not so unenviable.

The pioneer work of the Supreme Court in constitutional interpretation has, for all but special

[1] Flanders, *The Lives and Times of the Chief-Justices of the Supreme Court*, vol. II, p. 38.

students, fallen into something like obscurity owing to the luster of Marshall's achievements and to his habit of deciding cases without much reference to precedent. But these early labors are by no means insignificant, especially since they pointed the way to some of Marshall's most striking decisions. In Chisholm *vs.* Georgia,[1] which was decided in 1793, the Court ruled, in the face of an assurance in the *Federalist* to the contrary, that an individual might sue a State; and though this decision was speedily disallowed by resentful debtor States by the adoption of the Eleventh Amendment, its underlying premise that, "as to the purposes of the Union, the States are not sovereign" remained untouched; and three years later the Court affirmed the supremacy of national treaties over conflicting state laws and so established a precedent which has never been disturbed.[2] Meantime the Supreme Court was advancing, though with notable caution, toward an assertion of the right to pass upon the constitutionality of acts of Congress. Thus in 1792, Congress ordered the judges while on circuit to pass upon pension claims, their determinations to be reviewable by the Secretary of the Treasury. In protests which they filed with the President, the

[1] 2 Dallas, 419. [2] Ware *vs.* Hylton, 3 *ib.*, 199.

judges stated the dilemma which confronted them: either the new duty was a judicial one or it was not; if the latter, they could not perform it, at least not in their capacity as judges; if the former, then their decisions were not properly reviewable by an executive officer.   Washington promptly sent the protests to Congress, whereupon some extremists raised the cry of impeachment; but the majority hastened to amend the Act so as to meet the views of the judges.[1]   Four years later, in the Carriage Tax case,[2] the only question argued before the Court was that of the validity of a congressional excise.   Yet as late as 1800 we find Justice Samuel Chase of Maryland, who had succeeded Blair in 1795, expressing skepticism as to the right of the Court to disallow acts of Congress on the ground of their unconstitutionality, though at the same time admitting that the prevailing opinion among bench and bar supported the claim.

The great lack of the Federal Judiciary during these early years, and it eventually proved well-nigh fatal, was one of leadership.   Jay was a satisfactory magistrate, but he was not a great force on the Supreme Bench, partly on account of his peculiarities of temperament and his ill

[1] See 2 Dallas, 409.   [2] Hylton *vs.* United States, 3 Dallas, 171.

health, and partly because, even before he resigned in 1795 to run for Governor in New York, his
judicial career had been cut short by an important
diplomatic assignment to England. His successor,
Oliver Ellsworth, also suffered from ill health, and
he too was finally sacrificed on the diplomatic al-
tar by being sent to France in 1799. During the
same interval there were also several resignations
among the associate justices. So, what with its
shifting personnel, the lack of business, and the
brief semiannual terms, the Court secured only a
feeble hold on the imagination of the country. It
may be thought, no doubt, that judges anxious to
steer clear of politics did not require leadership in
the political sense. But the truth of the matter is
that willy-nilly the Federal Judiciary at this period
was bound to enter politics, and the only question
was with what degree of tact and prudence this
should be done. It was to be to the glory of Marshall that he recognized this fact perfectly and with
mingled boldness and caution grasped the leadership which the circumstances demanded.

The situation at the beginning was precarious
enough. While the Constitution was yet far from
having commended itself to the back country
democracy, that is, to the bulk of the American

people, the normal duties of the lower Federal Courts brought the judges into daily contact with prevalent prejudices and misconceptions in their most aggravated forms. Between 1790 and 1800 there were two serious uprisings against the new Government: the Whisky Rebellion of 1794 and Fries's Rebellion five years later. During the same period the popular ferment caused by the French Revolution was at its height. Entrusted with the execution of the laws, the young Judiciary "was necessarily thrust forward to bear the brunt in the first instance of all the opposition levied against the federal head," its revenue measures, its commercial restrictions, its efforts to enforce neutrality and to quell uprisings. In short, it was the point of attrition between the new system and a suspicious, excited populace.

Then, to make bad matters worse, Congress in 1798 passed the Sedition Act. Had political discretion instead of party venom governed the judges, it is not unlikely that they would have seized the opportunity presented by this measure to declare it void and by doing so would have made good their censorship of acts of Congress with the approval of even the Jeffersonian opposition. Instead, they enforced the Sedition Act, often with gratuitous rigor, while some of them even entertained prosecutions under a supposed Common Law of the United States. The immediate sequel to their action was the claim put forth in the Virginia and Kentucky Resolutions that the final authority in interpreting the National Constitution lay with the local legislatures. Before the principle of judicial review was supported by a single authoritative decision, it had thus become a partisan issue![1]

A few months later Jefferson was elected President, and the Federalists, seeing themselves about to lose control of the Executive and Congress, proceeded to take steps to convert the Judiciary into an avowedly partisan stronghold. By the Act of February 13, 1801, the number of associate justiceships was reduced to four, in the hope that the new Administration might in this way be excluded from the opportunity of making any appointments to the Supreme Bench, the number of district judgeships was enlarged by five, and six Circuit Courts were created which furnished places for sixteen more new judges. When John Adams, the retiring President, proceeded with the aid of the Federalist majority in the Senate

[1] See Herman V. Ames, *State Documents on Federal Relations*, Nos. 7-15

and of his Secretary of State, John Marshall, to fill up the new posts with the so-called "midnight judges,"[1] the rage and consternation of the Republican leaders broke all bounds. The Federal Judiciary, declared John Randolph, had become "an hospital of decayed politicians." Others pictured the country as reduced, under the weight of "supernumerary judges" and hosts of attendant lawyers, to the condition of Egypt under the Mamelukes. Jefferson's concern went deeper. "They have retired into the judiciary as a stronghold," he wrote Dickinson. "There the remains of Federalism are to be preserved and fed from the Treasury, and from that battery all the works of Republicanism are to be beaten down and destroyed." The Federal Judiciary, as a coördinate and independent branch of the Government, was confronted with a fight for life!

Meanwhile, late in November, 1800, Ellsworth had resigned, and Adams had begun casting about for his successor. First he turned to Jay, who declined on the ground that the Court, "under a system so defective," would never "obtain the

---

[1] So called because the appointment of some of them was supposed to have taken place as late as midnight, or later, of March 3–4, 1801. The supposition, however, was without foundation.

energy, weight, and dignity which were essential to its affording due support to the National Government, nor acquire the public confidence and respect which, as the last resort of the justice of the nation, it should possess." Adams now bethought himself of his Secretary of State and, without previously consulting him, on January 20, 1801, sent his name to the Senate. A week later the Senate ratified the nomination, and on the 4th of February Marshall accepted the appointment. The task despaired of by Jay and abandoned by Ellsworth was at last in capable hands.

CHAPTER II

MARSHALL'S EARLY YEARS

JOHN MARSHALL was born on September 24, 1755, in Fauquier County, Virginia. Though like Jefferson he was descended on his mother's side from the Randolphs of Turkey Island, colonial grandees who were also progenitors of John Randolph, Edmund Randolph, and Robert E. Lee, his father, Thomas Marshall, was "a planter of narrow fortune" and modest lineage and a pioneer. Fauquier was then on the frontier, and a few years after John was born the family moved still farther westward to a place called "The Hollow," a small depression on the eastern slope of the Blue Ridge. The external furnishings of the boy's life were extremely primitive, a fact which Marshall used later to recall by relating that his mother and sisters used thorns for buttons and that hot mush flavored with balm leaf was regarded as a very special dish. Neighbors, of course, were few and far between, but society was not lacking for all that. As the first of fifteen children, all of whom reached maturity, John found ample opportunity to cultivate that affectionate helpfulness and gayety of spirit which in after years even enemies accounted one of his most notable traits.

Among the various influences which, during the plastic years of boyhood and youth, went to shape the outlook of the future Chief Justice high rank must be accorded his pioneer life. It is not merely that the spirit of the frontier, with its independence of precedent and its audacity of initiative, breathes through his great constitutional decisions, but also that in being of the frontier Marshall escaped being something else. Had he been born in lowland Virginia, he would have imbibed the intense localism and individualism of the great plantation, and with his turn of mind might well have filled the rôle of Calhoun instead of that very different rôle he actually did fill. There was, indeed, one great planter with whom young Marshall was thrown into occasional contact, and that was his father's patron and patron saint, Washington. The appeal made to the lad's imagination by the great Virginian was deep and abiding. And it goes without saying that the horizons suggested by the fame of

Fort Venango and Fort Duquesne were not those of seaboard Virginia but of America.

Many are the great men who have owed their debt to a mother's loving helpfulness and alert understanding. Marshall, on the other hand, was his father's child. "My father," he was wont to declare in after years, "was a far abler man than any of his sons. To him I owe the solid foundations of all my success in life." What were these solid foundations? One was a superb physical constitution; another was a taste for intellectual delights; and to the upbuilding of both these in his son, Thomas Marshall devoted himself with enthusiasm and masculine good sense, aided on the one hand by a very select library consisting of Shakespeare, Milton, Dryden, and Pope, and on the other by the ever fresh invitation of the mountainside to health-giving sports.

Pope was the lad's especial textbook, and we are told that he had transcribed the whole of the *Essay on Man* by the time he was twelve and some of the *Moral Essays* as well, besides having "committed to memory many of the most interesting passages of that distinguished poet." The result is to be partially discerned many years later in certain tricks of Marshall's style; but indeed the influence of the great moralist must have penetrated far deeper. The *Essay on Man* filled, we may surmise, much the same place in the education of the first generation of American judges that Herbert Spencer's *Social Statics* filled in that of the judges of a later day. The *Essay on Man* pictures the universe as a species of constitutional monarchy governed "not by partial but by general laws"; in "man's imperial race" this beneficent sway expresses itself in two principles, "self-love to urge, and reason to restrain"; instructed by reason, self-love lies at the basis of all human institutions, the state, government, laws, and has "found the private in the public good"; so, on the whole, justice is the inevitable law of life. "Whatever is, is right." It is interesting to suppose that while Marshall was committing to memory the complacent lines of the *Essay on Man*, his cousin Jefferson may have been deep in the *Essay on the Origin of Inequality*.

At the age of fourteen Marshall was placed for a few months under the tuition of a clergyman named Campbell, who taught him the rudiments of Latin and introduced him to Livy, Cicero, and Horace. A little later the great debate over American rights burst forth and became with Marshall, as with so many promising lads of the time, the decisive factor in determining his intellectual bent, and he now began reading Blackstone. The great British orators, however, whose eloquence had so much to do, for instance, with shaping Webster's genius, came too late to influence him greatly.

The part which the War of Independence had in shaping the ideas and the destiny of John Marshall was most important. As the news of Lexington and Bunker Hill passed the Potomac, he was among the first to spring to arms. His services at the siege of Norfolk, the battles of Brandywine, Germantown, and Monmouth, and his share in the rigors of Valley Forge and in the capture of Stony Point, made him an American before he had ever had time to become a Virginian. As he himself wrote long afterwards: "I had grown up at a time when the love of the Union and the resistance to Great Britain were the inseparable inmates of the same bosom; . . . when the maxim 'United we stand, divided we fall' was the maxim of every orthodox American. And I had imbibed these sentiments so thoroughly that they constituted a part of my being. I carried them with me into the army, where I found myself associated with brave men from different States, who were risking life and everything valuable in a common cause believed by all to be most precious, and where I was confirmed in the habit of considering America as my country and Congress as my government."

Love of country, however, was not the only quality which soldiering developed in Marshall. The cheerfulness and courage which illuminated his patriotism brought him popularity among men. Though but a lieutenant, he was presently made a deputy judge advocate. In this position he displayed notable talent in adjusting differences between officers and men and also became acquainted with Washington's brilliant young secretary, Alexander Hamilton.

While still in active service in 1780, Marshall attended a course of law lectures given by George Wythe at William and Mary College. He owed this opportunity to Jefferson, who was then Governor of the State and who had obtained the abolition of the chair of divinity at the college and the introduction of a course in law and another in medicine. Whether the future Chief Justice was prepared to take full advantage of the opportunity thus offered is, however, a question. He had just fallen heels over head in love with Mary Ambler, whom three years later he married, and his notebook seems to show us that his thoughts were quite as much upon his sweetheart as upon the lecturer's wisdom.

None the less, as soon as the Courts of Virginia reopened, upon the capitulation of Cornwallis, Marshall hung out his shingle at Richmond and began the practice of his profession. The new capital was still hardly more than an outpost on the frontier, and conditions of living were rude in the extreme. "The Capitol itself," we are told, "was an ugly structure — 'a mere wooden barn' — on an unlovely site at the foot of a hill. The private dwellings scattered about were poor, mean, little wooden houses." "Main Street was still unpaved, deep with dust when dry and so muddy during a rainy season that wagons sank up to the axles." It ended in gullies and swamps. Trade, which was still in the hands of the British merchants, involved for the most part transactions in skins, furs, ginseng, snakeroot, and "dried rattlesnakes — used to make a viper broth for consumptive patients." "There was but one church building and attendance was scanty and infrequent." Not so, however, of Farmicola's tavern, whither card playing, drinking, and ribaldry drew crowds, especially when the legislature was in session.[1]

[1] Beveridge, vol. I, pp. 171–73.

But there was one institution of which Richmond could boast, even in comparison with New York, Boston, or Philadelphia, and that was its Bar. Randolph, Wickham, Campbell, Call, Pendleton, Wythe — these are names whose fame still survives wherever the history of the American Bar is cherished; and it was with their living bearers that young Marshall now entered into competition. The result is somewhat astonishing at first consideration, for even by the standards of his own day, when digests, indices, and the other numerous aids which now ease the path of the young attorney were generally lacking, his preparation had been slight. Several circumstances, however, came to his rescue. So soon after the Revolution British precedents were naturally rather out of favor, while on the other hand many of the questions which found their way into the courts were those peculiar to a new country and so were without applicable precedents for their solution. What was chiefly demanded of an attorney in this situation was a capacity for attention, the ability to analyze an opponent's argument, and a discerning eye for fundamental issues. Competent observers soon made the discovery that young Marshall possessed all these faculties to a marked degree and, what was just as important, his modesty made recognition by his elders easy and gracious.

From 1782 until the adoption of the Constitution, Marshall was almost continuously a member of the Virginia Legislature. He thus became a witness of that course of policy which throughout this period daily rendered the state governments more and more "the hope of their enemies, the despair of their friends." The termination of hostilities against England had relaxed the already feeble bonds connecting the States. Congress had powers which were only recommendatory, and its recommendations were ignored by the local legislatures. The army, unpaid and frequently in actual distress, was so rapidly losing its morale that it might easily become a prey to demagogues. The treaties of the new nation were flouted by every State in the Union. Tariff wars and conflicting land grants embittered the relations of sister States. The foreign trade of the country, it was asserted, "was regulated, taxed, monopolized, and crippled at the pleasure of the maritime powers of Europe." Burdened with debts which were the legacy of an era of speculation, a considerable part of the population, especially of the farmer class, was demanding measures of relief which threatened the

3

security of contracts. "Laws suspending the collection of debts, insolvent laws, instalment laws,
tender laws, and other expedients of a like nature, were familiarly adopted or openly and boldly
vindicated."[1]

From the outset Marshall ranged himself on the
side of that party in the Virginia Legislature which,
under the leadership of Madison, demanded with
growing insistence a general and radical constitutional reform designed at once to strengthen the
national power and to curtail state legislative
power. His attitude was determined not only by
his sympathy for the sufferings of his former com-
rades in arms and by his veneration for his father
and for Washington, who were of the same party,
but also by his military experience, which had rendered the pretensions of state sovereignty ridicu-
lous in his eyes. Local discontent came to a head
in the autumn of 1786 with the outbreak of Shays's
Rebellion in western Massachusetts. Marshall,
along with the great body of public men of the day,
conceived for the movement the gravest alarm, and
the more so since he considered it as the natural

---

[1] This review of conditions under the later Confederation is taken
from Story's *Discourse*, which is in turn based, at this point, on Marshall's *Life of Washington* and certain letters of his to Story.

culmination of prevailing tendencies.   In a letter
to James Wilkinson early in 1787, he wrote: "These
violent . . . dissensions in a State I had thought
inferior in wisdom and virtue to no one in our
Union, added to the strong tendency which the politics of many eminent characters among ourselves
have to promote private and public dishonesty,
cast a deep shade over that bright prospect which
the Revolution in America and the establishment of
our free governments had opened to the votaries of
liberty throughout the globe.   I fear, and there is
no opinion more degrading to the dignity of man,
that those have truth on their side who say that
man is incapable of governing himself."

Marshall accordingly championed the adoption
of the Constitution of 1787 quite as much because
of its provisions for diminishing the legislative powers of the States in the interest of private rights as
because of its provisions for augmenting the powers
of the General Government.   His attitude is revealed, for instance, in the opening words of his
first speech on the floor of the Virginia Convention,
to which he had been chosen a member from Richmond: "Mr. Chairman, I conceive that the object
of the discussion now before us is whether democracy or despotism be most eligible. . . .   The

supporters of the Constitution claim the title of being firm friends of liberty and the rights of man. . . . We prefer this system because we think it a well-regulated democracy. . . . What are the favorite maxims of democracy? A strict observance of justice and public faith. . . . Would to Heaven that these principles had been observed under the present government. Had this been the case the friends of liberty would not be willing now to part with it." The point of view which Marshall here assumed was obviously the same as that from which Madison, Hamilton, Wilson, and others on the floor of the Federal Convention had freely predicted that republican liberty must disappear from the earth unless the abuses of it practiced in many of the States could be eliminated.

Marshall's services in behalf of the Constitution in the closely fought battle for ratification which took place in the Virginia Convention are only partially disclosed in the pages of Elliot's *Debates*. He was already coming to be regarded as one excellent in council as well as in formal discussion, and his democratic manners and personal popularity with all classes were a pronounced asset for any cause he chose to espouse. Marshall's part on the floor of the Convention was, of course, much less conspicuous

than that of either Madison or Randolph, but in the second rank of the Constitution's defenders, including men like Corbin, Nicholas, and Pendleton, he stood foremost. His remarks were naturally shaped first of all to meet the immediate necessities of the occasion, but now and then they foreshadow views of a more enduring value. For example, he met a favorite contention of the opposition by saying that arguments based on the assumption that necessary powers would be abused were arguments against government in general and "a recommendation of anarchy." To Henry's despairing cry that the proposed system lacked checks, he replied: "What has become of his enthusiastic eulogium of the American spirit? We should find a check and control, when oppressed, from that source. In this country there is no exclusive personal stock of interest. The interest of the community is blended and inseparably connected with that of the individual. . . . When we consult the common good, we consult our own." And when Henry argued that a vigorous union was unnecessary because "we are separated by the sea from the powers of Europe," Marshall replied: "Sir, the sea makes them neighbors of us."

It is worthy of note that Marshall gave his great-est attention to the judiciary article as it appeared in the proposed Constitution. He pointed out that the principle of judicial independence was here better safeguarded than in the Constitution of Virginia. He stated in one breath the principle of judicial review and the doctrine of enumerated powers. If, said he, Congress "make a law not warranted by any of the powers enumerated, it would be considered by the judges as an infringe-ment of the Constitution which they are to guard; they would not consider such a law as coming with-in their jurisdiction. They would declare it void."[1] On the other hand, Marshall scoffed at the idea that the citizen of a State might bring an original action against another State in the Supreme Court. His dissections of Mason's and Henry's arguments frequently exhibit controversial skill of a high or-der. From Henry, indeed, Marshall drew a nota-ble tribute to his talent, which was at the same time proof of his ability to keep friends with his enemies.

[1] J. Elliot, *Debates* (Edition of 1836), vol. III, p. 503.   As to Bills of Rights, however, Marshall expressed the opinion that they were meant to be " merely recommendatory. Were it otherwise, . . . many laws which are found convenient would be unconstitutional." *Op. cit.*, vol. III, p. 509.

On the day the great Judiciary Act became law, Marshall attained his thirty-fourth year. His stride toward professional and political prominence was now rapid. At the same time his private interests were becoming more closely interwoven with his political principles and personal affiliations, and his talents were maturing. Hitherto his outlook upon life had been derived largely from older men, but his own individuality now began to assert itself; his groove in life was taking final shape.

The best description of Marshall shows him in the prime of his manhood a few months after his accession to the Supreme Bench. It appears in William Wirt's celebrated *Letters of the British Spy:*

The [Chief Justice] of the United States is, in his person, tall, meager, emaciated; his muscles relaxed, and his joints so loosely connected, as not only to disqualify him, apparently for any vigorous exertion of body, but to destroy everything like elegance and harmony in his air and movements. Indeed, in his whole appearance, and demeanour; dress, attitudes, gesture; sitting, standing or walking; he is as far removed from the idolized graces of Lord Chesterfield, as any other gentleman on earth. To continue the portrait: his head and face are small in proportion to his height; his complexion swarthy; the muscles of his face, being relaxed, give him the appearance of a man of fifty years of age, nor can he be much younger; his countenance has a faithful expression of great good humour and hilarity; while his black eyes — that unerring index — possess an irradiating spirit, which proclaims the imperial powers of the mind that sits enthroned within.

The "British Spy" then describes Marshall's personality as an orator at the time when he was still practicing at the Virginia bar:

His voice [the description continues] is dry and hard; his attitude, in his most effective orations, was often extremely awkward, as it was not unusual for him to stand with his left foot in advance, while all his gestures proceeded from his right arm, and consisted merely in a vehement, perpendicular swing of it from about the elevation of his head to the bar, behind which he was accustomed to stand. . . . [Nevertheless] if eloquence may be said to consist in the power of seizing the attention with irresistible force, and never permitting it to elude the grasp until the hearer has received the conviction which the speaker intends, [then] this extraordinary man, without the aid of fancy, without the advantages of person, voice, attitude, gesture, or any of the ornaments of an orator, deserves to be considered as one of the most eloquent men in the world. . . . He possesses one original, and, almost, supernatural faculty; the faculty of developing a subject by a single glance of his mind, and detecting at once, the very point on which every controversy depends. No matter what the question; though ten times more knotty than the gnarled oak, the lightning of heaven is not more rapid nor more resistless, than his astonishing penetration. Nor does

the exercise of it seem to cost him an effort.   On the contrary, it is as easy as vision.   I am persuaded that his
eyes do not fly over a landscape and take in its various
objects with more promptitude and facility, than his
mind embraces and analyzes the most complex subject.

Possessing while at the bar this intellectual elevation,
which enables him to look down and comprehend the
whole ground at once, he determined immediately and
without difficulty, on which side the question might be
most advantageously approached and assailed.   In a
bad cause his art consisted in laying his premises so
remotely from the point directly in debate, or else in
terms so general and so spacious, that the hearer, seeing
no consequence which could be drawn from them, was
just as willing to admit them as not; but his premises
once admitted, the demonstration, however distant, followed as certainly, as cogently, as inevitably, as any
demonstration in Euclid.

All his eloquence consists in the apparently deep self-
conviction, and emphatic earnestness of his manner, the
correspondent simplicity and energy of his style; the
close and logical connexion of his thoughts; and the easy
gradations by which he opens his lights on the attentive
minds of his hearers.

The audience are never permitted to pause for a moment.   There is no stopping to weave garlands of flowers, to hang in festoons, around a favorite argument.
On the contrary, every sentence is progressive; every
idea sheds new light on the subject; the listener is kept
perpetually in that sweetly pleasurable vibration, with
which the mind of man always receives new truths; the
dawn advances in easy but unremitting pace; the subject opens gradually on the view; until, rising in high

relief, in all its native colors and proportions, the argument is consummated by the conviction of the delighted hearer.

What appeared to Marshall's friends as most likely in his early middle years to stand in the way of his advancement was his addiction to ease and to a somewhat excessive conviviality. But it is worth noting that the charge of conviviality was never repeated after he was appointed Chief Justice; and as to his unstudious habits, therein perhaps lay one of the causes contributing to his achievement. Both as attorney and as judge, he preferred the quest of broad, underlying principles, and, with plenty of time for recuperation from each exertion, he was able to bring to each successive task undiminished vitality and unclouded attention. What the author of the *Leviathan* remarks of himself may well be repeated of Marshall — that he made more use of his brains than of his bookshelves and that, if he had read as much as most men, he would have been as ignorant as they.

That Marshall was one of the leading members of his profession in Virginia, the most recent biographical researches unmistakably prove. "From 1790 until his election to Congress nine years later," Albert J. Beveridge[1] writes, "Marshall argued 113 cases decided by the court of appeals of Virginia. . . . He appeared during this time in practically every important cause heard and determined by the supreme tribunal of the State." Practically all this litigation concerned property rights, and much of it was exceedingly intricate. Marshall's biographer also points out the interesting fact that "whenever there was more than one attorney for the client who retained Marshall, the latter almost invariably was retained to make the closing argument." He was thus able to make good any lack of knowledge of the technical issues involved as well as to bring his great debating powers to bear with the best advantage.

Meanwhile Marshall was also rising into political prominence. From the first a supporter of Washington's Administration, he was gradually thrust into the position of Federalist leader in Virginia. In 1794 he declined the post of Attorney-General, which Washington had offered him. In the following year he became involved in the acrimonious struggle over the Jay Treaty with Great Britain, and both in the Legislature and before meetings of citizens defended the treaty so aggressively that its

[1] *The Life of John Marshall,* vol. II, p. 177.

opponents were finally forced to abandon their contention that it was unconstitutional and to content themselves with a simple denial that it was expedient.   Early in 1796 Marshall made his first appearance before the Supreme Court, in the case of Ware *vs.* Hylton.   The fame of his defense of "the British Treaty" during the previous year had preceded him, and his reception by the Federalist leaders from New York and New England was notably cordial.   His argument before the Court, too, though it did not in the end prevail, added greatly to his reputation.   "His head," said Rufus King, who heard the argument, "is one of the best organized of any one that I have known."

Either in 1793 or early in the following year, Marshall participated in a business transaction which, though it did not impart to his political and constitutional views their original bent, yet must have operated more or less to confirm his opinions.   A syndicate composed of Marshall, one of his brothers, and two other gentlemen, purchased from the British heirs what remained of the great Fairfax estate in the Northern Neck, a tract "embracing over 160,000 acres of the best land in Virginia."   By an Act passed during the Revolution, Virginia had decreed the confiscation of all lands held by

British subjects; and though the State had never prosecuted the forfeiture of this particular estate, she was always threatening to do so. Marshall's investment thus came to occupy for many years a precarious legal footing which, it may be surmised, did not a little to keep alert his natural sympathy for all victims of legislative oppression. Moreover the business relation which he formed with Robert Morris in financing the investment brought him into personal contact for the first time with the interests behind Hamilton's financial program, the constitutionality of which he had already defended on the hustings.

It was due also to this business venture that Marshall was at last persuaded to break through his rule of declining office and to accept appointment in 1797, together with Pinckney and Gerry, on the famous "X.Y.Z." mission to France. From this single year's employment he obtained nearly $20,000, which, says his biographer, "over and above his expenses," was "three times his annual earnings at the bar"; and the money came just in the nick of time to save the Fairfax investment, for Morris was now bankrupt and in jail. But not less important as a result of his services was the enhanced reputation which Marshall's correspondence with Talleyrand brought him. His return to Philadelphia was a popular triumph, and even Jefferson, temporarily discomfited by the "X.Y.Z." disclosures, found it discreet to go through the form of paying him court — whereby hangs a tale. Jefferson called at Marshall's tavern. Marshall was out. Jefferson thereupon left a card deploring how "unlucky" he had been. Commenting years afterwards upon the occurrence, Marshall remarked that this was one time at least when Jefferson came *near* telling the truth.

Through the warm insistence of Washington, Marshall was finally persuaded in the spring of 1799 to stand as Federalist candidate for Congress in the Richmond district. The expression of his views at this time is significant. A correspondent of an Alexandria newspaper signing himself "Freeholder" put to him a number of questions intended to call forth Marshall's opinions on the issues of the day. In answering a query as to whether he favored an alliance with Great Britain, the candidate declared that the whole of his "politics respecting foreign nations" was "reducible to this single position. . . . Commercial intercourse with all, but political ties with none." But a more pressing issue on which the public wished information was that furnished by the Alien and Sedition laws, which Marshall had originally criticized on grounds both of expediency and of constitutionality. Now, however, he defended these measures on constitutional grounds, taking the latitudinarian position that "powers necessary for the attainment of all objects which are general in their nature, which interest all America . . . would be naturally vested in the Government of the whole," but he declared himself strongly opposed to their renewal. At the same time he denounced the Virginia Resolutions as calculated "to sap the foundations of our Union."

The election was held late in April, under conditions which must have added greatly to popular interest. Following the custom in Virginia, the voter, instead of casting a ballot, merely declared his preference in the presence of the candidates, the election officials, and the assembled multitude. In the intensity of the struggle no voter, halt, lame, or blind, was overlooked; and a barrel of whisky near at hand lent further zest to the occasion. Time and again the vote in the district was a tie, and as a result frequent personal encounters took place between aroused partisans. Marshall's election by a narrow majority in a borough which was strongly pro-Jeffersonian was due, indeed, not to his principles but to his personal popularity and to the support which he received from Patrick Henry, the former Governor of the State.

The most notable event of his brief stay in Congress was his successful defense of President Adams's action in handing over to the British authorities, in conformity with the twenty-seventh article of the Jay treaty, Jonathan Robins, who was alleged to be a fugitive from justice. Adams's critics charged him with having usurped a judicial function. "The President," said Marshall in reply, "is sole organ of the nation in its external relations, and its sole representative with foreign nations. Of consequence, the demand of a foreign nation can only be made on him. He possesses the whole executive power. He holds and directs the force of the nation. Of consequence, any act to be performed by the force of the nation is to be performed through him. He is charged to execute the laws. A treaty is declared to be a law. He must then execute a treaty where he, and he alone, possesses the means of executing it." This is one of the few speeches ever uttered on the floor of Congress which demonstrably made votes. Gallatin, who had been set to answer Marshall, threw up his brief; and the resolutions against the President were defeated by a House hostile to him.

Marshall's course in Congress was characterized throughout by independence of character, moderation of views, and level good sense, of which his various congressional activities afford abundant evidence. Though he had himself been one of the "X.Y.Z." mission, Marshall now warmly supported Adams's policy of renewing diplomatic relations with France. He took his political life in his hands to register a vote against the Sedition Act, a proposal to repeal which was brought before the House. He foiled a scheme which his party associates had devised, in view of the approaching presidential election, to transfer to a congressional committee the final authority in canvassing the electoral vote — a plan all too likely to precipitate civil war. His Federalist brethren of the extreme Hamiltonian type quite resented the frequency with which he was wont to kick over the party traces. "He is disposed," wrote Sedgwick, the Speaker, "to express great respect for the sovereign people and to quote their opinions as an evidence of truth," which "is of all things the most destructive of personal independence and of that weight of character which a great man ought to possess."[1]

Marshall had now come to be practically indispensable to the isolated President, at whose most earnest insistence he entered the Cabinet as Secretary of State, though he had previously declined to become Secretary of War. The presidential campaign was the engrossing interest of the year, and as it spread its "havoc of virulence" throughout the country, Federalists of both factions seemed to turn to Marshall in the hope that, by some miracle of conciliation, he could save the day. The hope proved groundless, however, and all that was ultimately left the party which had founded the Government was to choose a President from the rival leaders of the opposition. Of these Marshall preferred Burr, because, as he explained, he knew Jefferson's principles better. Besides having foreign prejudices, Mr. Jefferson, he continued, "appears to me to be a man who will embody himself with the House of Representatives, and by weakening the office of President, he will increase his personal power." Better political prophecy has, indeed, rarely been penned. Deferring nevertheless to Hamilton's insistence — and, as events were to

[1] Letter from Sedgwick to King, May 11, 1800. *Life and Correspondence of Rufus King*, vol. III, pp. 236-7.

prove, to his superior wisdom — Marshall kept aloof from the fight in the House, and his implacable foe was elected.

Marshall was already one of the eminent men of the country when Adams, without consulting him, nominated him for Chief Justice. He stood at the head of the Virginia bar; he was the most generally trusted leader of his party; he already had a national reputation as an interpreter of the Constitution. Yet his appointment as Chief Justice aroused criticism even among his party friends. Their doubt did not touch his intellectual attainments, but in their opinion his political moderation, his essential democracy, his personal amiability, all counted against him. "He is," wrote Sedgwick, "a man of very affectionate disposition, of great simplicity of manners, and honest and honorable in all his conduct. He is attached to pleasures, with convivial habits strongly fixed. He is indolent therefore. He has a strong attachment to popularity but is indisposed to sacrifice to it his integrity; hence he is disposed on all popular subjects to feel the public pulse, and hence results indecision and *an expression* of doubt."[1]

It was perhaps fortunate for the Federal Judi-

[1] *Op. cit.*

ciary, of which he was now to take command, that John Marshall was on occasion "disposed . . . to feel the public pulse." A headstrong pilot might speedily have dashed his craft on the rocks; a timid one would have abandoned his course; but Marshall did neither. The better answer to Sedgwick's fears was given in 1805 when John Randolph declared that Marshall's "real worth was never known until he was appointed Chief Justice." And Sedgwick is further confuted by the portraits of the Chief Justice, which, with all their diversity, are in accord on that stubborn chin, that firm placid mouth, that steady, benignant gaze, so capable of putting attorneys out of countenance when they had to face it overlong. Here are the lineaments of self-confidence unmarred by vanity, of dignity without condescension, of tenacity untouched by fanaticism, and above all, of an easy conscience and unruffled serenity. It required the lodestone of a great and thoroughly congenial responsibility to bring to light Marshall's real metal.

CHAPTER III

BY a singular coincidence Marshall took his seat as Chief Justice at the opening of the first term of Court in Washington, the new capital, on Wednesday, February 4, 1801. The most beautiful of capital cities was then little more than a swamp, athwart which ran a streak of mire named by solemn congressional enactment "Pennsylvania Avenue." At one end of this difficult thoroughfare stood the President's mansion — still in the hands of the builders but already sagging and leaking through the shrinkage of the green timber they had used — two or three partially constructed office-buildings, and a few private edifices and boarding houses. Marshall never removed his residence to Washington but occupied chambers in one or other of these buildings, in company with some of the associate justices. This arrangement was practicable owing to the brevity of the judicial term, which usually lasted little more than six weeks, and was almost necessitated by the unhealthful climate of the place. It may be conjectured that the life of John Marshall was prolonged for some years by the Act of 1802, which abolished the August term of court, for in the late summer and early autumn the place swarmed with mosquitoes and reeked with malaria.

The Capitol, which stood at the other end of Pennsylvania Avenue, was in 1801 even less near completion than the President's house; at this time the south wing rose scarcely twenty feet above its foundations. In the north wing, which was nearer completion, in a basement chamber, approached by a small hall opening on the eastern side of the Capitol and flanked by pillars carved to represent bundles of cornstalks with ears half opened at the top, Marshall held court for more than a third of a century and elaborated his great principles of constitutional law. This room, untouched by British vandalism in the invasion of 1814, was christened by the witty malignity of John Randolph, "the cave of Trophonius."[1]

---

[1] It should, however, be noted in the interest of accuracy, that the Court does not seem to have occupied its basement chamber during the years 1814 to 1818, while the Capitol was under repair.

It was in the Senate Chamber in this same north wing that Marshall administered the oath of office to Jefferson just one month after he himself had taken office. There have been in American history few more dramatic moments, few more significant, than this occasion when these two men confronted each other. They detested each other with a detestation rooted in the most essential differences of character and outlook. As good fortune arranged it, however, each came to occupy precisely that political station in which he could do his best work and from which he could best correct the bias of the other. Marshall's nationalism rescued American democracy from the vaguer horizons to which Jefferson's cosmopolitanism beckoned, and gave to it a secure abode with plenty of elbow-room. Jefferson's emphasis on the right of the contemporary majority to shape its own institutions prevented Marshall's constitutionalism from developing a privileged aristocracy. Marshall was finely loyal to principles accepted from others; Jefferson was speculative, experimental; the personalities of these two men did much to conserve essential values in the American Republic.

As Jefferson turned from his oath-taking to deliver his inaugural, Marshall must have listened with attentive ears for some hint of the attitude which the new Administration proposed to take with regard to the Federal Judiciary and especially with regard to the recent act increasing its numbers; but if so, he got nothing for his pains. The new President seemed particularly bent upon dispelling any idea that there was to be a political proscription. Let us, said he, "unite with one heart and one mind. Let us restore to social intercourse that harmony and affection without which liberty and even life itself are but dreary things. . . . Every difference of opinion is not a difference of principle. We have called by different names brethren of the same principle. We are all Republicans, we are all Federalists."

Notwithstanding the reassurance of these words, the atmosphere both of official Washington and of the country at large was electric with dangerous currents — dangerous especially to judges — and Jefferson was far too well known as an adept in the manipulation of political lightning to admit of much confidence that he would fail to turn these forces against his enemy when the opportune moment should arrive. The national courts were regarded with more distrust by the mass of Republicans than any other part of the hated system created by the once dominant Federalists. The reasons why this was so have already been indicated, but the most potent reason in 1801, because it was still freshest in mind, was the domineering part which the national judges had played in the enforcement of the Sedition Act. The terms of this illiberal measure made, and were meant to make, criticism of the party in power dangerous. The judges — Federalists to a man and bred, moreover, in a tradition which ill distinguished the office of judge from that of prosecutor — felt little call to mitigate the lot of those who fell within the toils of the law under this Act. A shining mark for the Republican enemies of the Judiciary was Justice Samuel Chase of the Supreme Court. It had fallen to Chase's lot to preside successively at the trial of Thomas Cooper for sedition, at the second trial of John Fries for treason, and at the trial of James Thompson Callender at Richmond for sedition. On each of the two latter occasions the defendant's counsel, charging "oppressive conduct" on the part of the presiding judge, had thrown up their briefs and rushed from the court room. In 1800 there were few Republicans who did not regard Chase as "the bloody Jeffreys of America."

Local conditions also frequently accentuated the prevailing prejudice against the Judiciary. The people of Kentucky, afraid that their badly tangled land titles were to be passed upon by the new Federal Courts, were already insisting, when Jefferson took office, that the Act of the 13th of February creating these courts be repealed. In Maryland extensive and radical alterations of the judicial system of the State were pending. In Pennsylvania the situation was even more serious, for though the judges of the higher courts of that commonwealth were usually men of ability, education, and character, the inferior magistrates were frequently the very opposite. By the state constitution judges were removable for serious offenses by impeachment, and for lesser reasons by the Governor upon the address of two-thirds of both branches of the Legislature. So long, however, as the Federalists had remained in power neither remedy had been applied; but in 1799, when the Republicans had captured both the governorship and the Legislature, a much needed purgation of the lower courts had forthwith begun.

Unfortunately this is a sort of reform that grows by what it feeds upon. Having got rid of the less fit members of the local judiciary, the Republican

leaders next turned their attention to some of their
aggressive party foes on the Superior Bench. The
most offensive of these was Alexander Addison,
president of one of the Courts of Common Pleas
of the State. He had started life as a Presby-
terian preacher and had found it natural to add
to his normal judicial duties the business of in-
culcating "sound morals and manners."[1] Addison had at once taken the Alien and Sedition laws
under his wing, though their enforcement did not
fall within his jurisdiction, and he found in the
progress of the French Revolution numerous texts
for partisan harangues to county juries. For some
reason Addison's enemies decided to resort to impeachment rather than to removal by address; and,
as a result, in January, 1803, the State Senate
found him guilty of "misdemeanor," ordered his
removal from office, and disqualified him for judicial office in Pennsylvania. Not long afterwards
the House of Representatives granted without inquiry or discussion a petition to impeach three members of the Supreme Court of the State for having

[1] President Dickinson of Pennsylvania wrote the Chief Justice and
judges of the Supreme Court of the Commonwealth, on October 8,
1785, that they ought not to content themselves merely with enforcing
the law, but should also endeavor to "inculcate sound morals and
manners." *Pennsylvania Archives*, vol. x, pp. 623-24.

punished one Thomas Passmore for contempt of court without a jury trial.

Jefferson entered office with his mind made up that the Act of the 13th of February should be repealed.[1] He lacked only a theory whereby he could reconcile this action with the Constitution, and that was soon forthcoming. According to the author of this theory, John Taylor of Caroline, a budding "Doctor Irrefragabilis" of the State Rights school, the proposed repeal raised two questions: first, whether Congress could abolish courts created by a previous act of Congress; and second, whether, with such courts abolished, their judges still retained office. Addressing himself to the first question, Taylor pointed out that the Act of the 13th of February had itself by instituting a new system abolished the then existing inferior courts. As to the second point, he wrote thus: "The Constitution declares that the judge shall hold his office during good behavior. Could it mean that he should hold office after it had been abolished? Could it mean that his tenure should be limited by behaving well in an office which did not exist?" A

---

[1] In this connection Mr. Beveridge draws my attention to Jefferson's letter to A. Stuart of April 5, 1801. See the *Complete Works of Jefferson* (Washington, 1857), vol. IV, p. 393.

construction based on such absurdities, said he, "overturns the benefits of language and intellect."

In his message of December 8, 1801, Jefferson gave the signal for the repeal of the obnoxious measure, and a month later Breckinridge of Kentucky introduced the necessary resolution in the Senate. In the prolonged debate which followed, the Republicans in both Senate and House rang the changes on Taylor's argument. The Federalists made a twofold answer. Some, accepting the Republican premise that the fate of the judge was necessarily involved with that of the court, denied *in toto* the validity of repeal. Gouverneur Morris, for instance, said: "You shall not take the man from the office but you may take the office from the man; you may not drown him, but you may sink his boat under him. . . . Is this not absurd?" Other Federalists, however, were ready to admit that courts of statutory origin could be abolished by statute but added that the operation of Congress's power in this connection was limited by the plain requirement of the Constitution that judges of the United States should hold office during good behavior. Hence, though a valid repeal of the Act in question would take from the judges the powers which they derived from its provisions, the repeal would still leave them judges of the United States until they died, resigned, or were legally removed in consequence of impeachment. The Federalist orators in general contended that the spirit of the Constitution confirmed its letter, and that its intention was clear that the national judges should pass finally upon the constitutionality of acts of Congress and should therefore be as secure as possible from legislative molestation.

The repeal of this Act was voted by a strict party majority and was reënforced by a provision postponing the next session of the Supreme Court until the following February. The Republican leaders evidently hoped that by that time all disposition to test the validity of the Repealing Act in the Court would have passed. But by this very precaution they implied a recognition of the doctrine of judicial review and the whole trend of the debate abundantly confirmed this implication. Breckinridge, Randolph, and Giles, it is true, scouted the claim made for the courts as "unheard-of doctrine," and as "mockery of the high powers of legislation"; but the rank and file of their followers, with the excesses of the French Revolution a recent memory and a "consolidated government" a recent fear, were not to be seduced from what they clearly regarded as established doctrine. Moreover, when it came to legislation concerning the Supreme Court, the majority of the Republicans again displayed genuine moderation, for, thrusting aside an obvious temptation to swamp that tribunal with additional judges of their own creed, they merely restored it to its original size under the Act of 1789.

Nevertheless the most significant aspect in the repeal of the Act of the 13th of February was the fact itself. The Republicans had not shown a more flagrant partisanism in effecting this repeal than had the Federalists in originally enacting the measure which was now at an end. Though the Federalists had sinned first, the fact nevertheless remained that in realizing their purpose the Republican majority had established a precedent which threatened to make of the lower Federal Judiciary the merest cat's-paw of party convenience. The attitude of the Republican leaders was even more menacing, for it touched the security of the Supreme Court itself in the enjoyment of its highest prerogative and so imperiled the unity of the nation. Beyond any doubt the moment was now at hand when the Court must prove to its supporters that it was still worth defending and to all that the Constitution had an authorized final interpreter.

Marshall's first constitutional case was that of Marbury *vs.* Madison.[1] The facts of this famous litigation are simple. On March 2, 1801, William Marbury had been nominated by President Adams to the office of Justice of the Peace in the District of Columbia for five years; his nomination had been ratified by the Senate; his commission had been signed and sealed; but it had not yet been delivered when Jefferson took office. The new President ordered Madison, his Secretary of State, not to deliver the commission. Marbury then applied to the Supreme Court for a writ of mandamus to the Secretary of State under the supposed authorization of the thirteenth section of the Act of 1789, which empowered the Court to issue the writ "in cases warranted by the principles and usages of law to . . . persons holding office under the authority of the United States." The Court at first took jurisdiction of the case and issued a rule to the Secretary of State ordering him to show cause, but it ultimately dismissed the suit for want of jurisdiction on the ground that the thirteenth section was unconstitutional.

Such are the lawyer's facts of the case; it is the

[1] 1 Cranch, 137. The following account of the case is drawn largely upon my *Doctrine of Judicial Review* (Princeton, 1914).

historian's facts about it which are today the interesting and instructive ones. Marshall, reversing the
usual order of procedure, left the question of jurisdiction till the very last, and so created for himself an opportunity to lecture the President on his
duty to obey the law and to deliver the commission. Marshall based his homily on the questionable assumption that the President had not the
power to remove Marbury from office, for if he had
this power the nondelivery of the document was of
course immaterial. Marshall's position was equally questionable when he contended that the thirteenth section violated that clause of Article III of
the Constitution which gives the Supreme Court
original jurisdiction "in all cases affecting ambassadors, other public ministers, and consuls, and
those in which a State shall be party." These
words, urged the Chief Justice, must be given an
exclusive sense "or they have no operation at all."
This position is quite untenable, for even when
given only their affirmative value these words still
place the cases enumerated beyond the reach of
Congress, and this may have been their only purpose. However, granting the Chief Justice his view
of Article III, still we are not forced to challenge
the validity of what Congress had done. For the

5

view taken a little later by the Court was that it was not the intention of Congress by this language to confer any jurisdiction at all, but only to give the right to issue the writ where the jurisdiction already existed. What the Court should have done, allowing its view of Article III to have been correct, was to dismiss the case as not falling within the contemplation of section thirteen, and not on the ground of the unconstitutionality of that section.

Marshall's opinion in Marbury *vs.* Madison was a political *coup* of the first magnitude, and by it he achieved half a dozen objects, some of the greatest importance. In the first place, while avoiding a direct collision with the executive power, he stigmatized his enemy Jefferson as a violator of the laws which as President he was sworn to support. Again, he evaded the perilous responsibility of passing upon the validity of the recent Repeal Act in quo warranto proceedings, such as were then being broached.[1] For if the Supreme Court could not

[1] See Benton's *Abridgment of the Debates of Congress*, vol. II, pp. 665–68. Marshall expressed the opinion in private that the repealing act was "operative in depriving the judges of all power derived from the act repealed" but not their office, "which is a mere capacity, without new appointment, to receive and exercise any new judicial power which the legislature may confer." Quoted by W. S. Carpenter in *American Political Science Review*, vol. IX, p. 528.

issue the writ of mandamus in suits begun in it by individuals, neither could it issue the writ of quo warranto in such suits. Yet again Marshall scored in exhibiting the Court in the edifying and reassuring light of declining, even from the hands of Congress, jurisdiction to which it was not entitled by the Constitution, an attitude of self-restraint which emphasized tremendously the Court's claim to the function of judicial review, now first definitely registered in deliberate judicial decision.

At this point in Marshall's handling of the case the consummate debater came to the assistance of the political strategist. Every one of his arguments in this opinion in support of judicial review will be found anticipated in the debate on the Repeal Act. What Marshall did was to gather these arguments together, winnow them of their trivialities, inconsistencies, and irrelevancies, and compress the residuum into a compact presentation of the case which marches to its conclusion with all the precision of a demonstration from Euclid.

The salient passages of this part of his opinion are the following:

[In the United States] the powers of the legislature are defined and limited; and that those limits may not be mistaken, or forgotten, the Constitution is written. To what purpose are powers limited, and to what purpose is that limitation committed in writing if these limits may, at any time, be passed by those intended to be restrained? The distinction between a government with limited and unlimited powers is abolished, if those limits do not confine the persons on which they are imposed, and if acts prohibited and acts allowed are of equal obligation. It is a proposition too plain to be contested: that the Constitution controls any legislative act repugnant to it; or, that the legislature may alter the Constitution by an ordinary act.

[If, then,] an act of the legislature, repugnant to the Constitution, is void, does it, notwithstanding its invalidity, bind the courts, and oblige them to give it effect? Or, in other words, though it be not law, does it constitute a rule as operative as if it was a law? This would be to overthrow in fact what was established in theory; and would seem, at first view, an absurdity too gross to be insisted on. It shall, however, receive a more attentive consideration.

It is emphatically the province and duty of the judicial department to say what the law is. Those who apply the rule to particular cases, must of necessity expound and interpret that rule. If two laws conflict with each other, the courts must decide on the operation of each. So if a law be in opposition to the Constitution; if both the law and the Constitution apply to a particular case, so that the court must either decide that case conformably to the law, disregarding the Constitution, or conformably to the Constitution, disregarding the law, the court must determine which of these conflicting rules governs the case. This is of the very essence of judicial duty.

[However, there are those who maintain] that courts must close their eyes on the Constitution, and see only the law. . . . This doctrine would subvert the very foundation of all written constitutions. It would declare that an act which, according to the principles and theory of our government, is entirely void, is yet, in practice, completely obligatory. It would declare that if the legislature shall do what is expressly forbidden, such act, notwithstanding the express prohibition, is in reality effectual.

[Moreover,] the peculiar expressions of the Constitution of the United States furnish additional arguments in favor of its rejection. The judicial power of the United States is extended to all cases arising under the Constitution. Could it be the intention of those who gave this power, to say that in using it the Constitution should not be looked into? That a case arising under the Constitution should be decided without examining the instrument under which it arises? This is too extravagant to be maintained.

In some cases, then, the Constitution must be looked into by the judges. And if they can open it at all, what part of it are they forbidden to read or to obey? There are many other parts of the Constitution which serve to illustrate this subject. . . . "No person," says the Constitution, "shall be convicted of treason unless on the testimony of two witnesses to the same overt act, or on confession in open court." Here the language of the Constitution is addressed especially to the courts. It prescribes, directly for them, a rule of evidence not to be departed from. If the legislature should change that rule, and declare one witness, or a confession out of court, sufficient for conviction, must the constitutional principle yield to the legislative act? . . .

It is also not entirely unworthy of observation, that in declaring what shall be the supreme law of the land, the Constitution itself is first mentioned; and not the laws of the United States generally, but those only which shall be made in pursuance of the Constitution, have that rank.

Thus, the particular phraseology of the Constitution of the United States confirms and strengthens the principle, supposed to be essential to all written constitutions, that a law repugnant to the Constitution is void; and that courts, as well as other departments are bound by that instrument.

There is not a false step in Marshall's argument. It is, for instance, not contended that the language of the Constitution establishes judicial review but only that it "confirms and strengthens the principle." Granting the finality of judicial decisions and that they may not be validly disturbed by legislative enactment, the argument is logically conclusive, whatever practical difficulties it may ignore.

Turning back to the case itself, we ought finally to note how Marshall utilized this opportunity to make manifest the newly found solidarity of the Court. For the first time in its history the Court was one voice, speaking through its Chief Justice the ineluctable decrees of the law. Ordinarily even Marshall would not have found this achievement an easy task, for there were difficult personalities among his associates. He had in Adams's Cabinet demonstrated his faculty "of putting his ideas into the minds of others, unconsciously to them," and of this power he now made use, as well as of the advantage to be obtained from the impending common danger.

The case of Marbury *vs.* Madison was decided on February 24, 1803, and therefore fell between two other events which were immediately of almost as great importance in the struggle now waxing over the judiciary. The first of these was the impeachment of Judge Pickering of the New Hampshire District Court, which was suggested by the President on the 3d of February and voted by the House on the 18th of February; the other was an address which Justice Chase delivered on the 2d of May to a Baltimore grand jury, assailing the repeal of the Judiciary Act and universal suffrage and predicting the deterioration of "our republican Constitution . . . into a mobocracy, the worst of all possible governments."[1] Considering the fact that the President was still smarting from the Chief Justice's lash and also that Chase himself was more

[1] The account here given of Chase's trial is based on Charles Evans's shorthand *Report* (Baltimore, 1805), supplemented by J. Q. Adams's *Memoirs*.

heartily detested by the Republicans than any other member of the Supreme Bench, nothing could have been more untimely than this fresh judicial excursion into the field of "manners and morals," and partisan malice was naturally alert to interpret it as something even more offensive. The report soon came from Baltimore that Chase had deliberately assailed the Administration as "weak, pusillanimous, relaxed," and governed by the sole desire of continuing "in unfairly acquired power." But even before this intelligence arrived, Jefferson had decided that the opportunity afforded by Chase's outburst was too good a one to be neglected. Writing on the 13th of May to Nicholson of Maryland, who already had Pickering's impeachment in charge, the President inquired: "Ought this seditious and official attack on the principles of our Constitution and the proceedings of a State go unpunished?" But he straightway added: "The question is for your consideration; for myself it is better I should not interfere."

Pickering's trial began on March 2, 1804, and had a bearing on Chase's fate which at once became clear. The evidence against the New Hampshire judge showed intoxication and profanity on the bench and entire unfitness for office, but further evidence introduced in his behalf proved the defendant's insanity; and so the question at once arose whether an insane man can be guilty of "high crimes and misdemeanors?" Greatly troubled by this new aspect of the case, the Senate none the less voted Pickering guilty "as charged," by the required two-thirds majority, though eight members refused to vote at all. But the exponents of "judge-breaking" saw only the action of the Senate and were blind to its hesitation. On the same day on which the Senate gave its verdict on Pickering, the House by a strictly partisan vote decreed Chase's impeachment.

The charges against Chase were finally elaborated in eight articles. The substance of the first six was that he had been guilty of "oppressive conduct" at the trials of John Fries and James Thompson Callender. The seventh charged him with having attempted at some time in 1800 to dragoon a grand jury at Newcastle, Delaware, into bringing forward an accusation of sedition against a local paper. These seven articles related therefore to transactions already four or five years old. The eighth article alone was based on the address at Baltimore, which it characterized as "an intemperate and inflammatory political harangue," delivered "with intent to excite the fears and resentment . . . of the good people of Maryland against their State Government and Constitution, . . . and against the Government of the United States."

But the charges framed against Chase revealed only imperfectly the animus which was now coming more and more to control the impeachers. Fortunately, however, there was one man among the President's advisers who was ready to carry the whole antijudicial program as far as possible. This uncompromising opponent was William Branch Giles, Senator from Virginia, whose views on the subject of impeachment were taken down by John Quincy Adams just as Chase's trial was about to open. Giles, according to this record, "treated with the utmost contempt the idea of an *independent judiciary* — said there was not a word about their independence in the Constitution. . . . The power of impeachment was given without limitation to the House of Representatives; the power of trying impeachment was given equally without limitation to the Senate; and if the Judges of the Supreme Court should dare, as they had done, to declare an act of Congress unconstitutional, or to send a mandamus to the Secretary of State, as they had done, it was the unreserved right of the House of Representatives to impeach them, and that of the Senate to remove them, for giving such opinions, however, honest or sincere they may have been in entertaining them." For "impeachment was not a criminal prosecution, it was no prosecution at all." It only signified that the impeached officer held dangerous opinions and that his office ought to be in better hands. "I perceive," adds Adams, on his own account, "that the impeachment system is to be pursued, and the whole bench of the Supreme Court to be swept away, because *their offices are w nted.* And in the present state of things I am convinced it is as easy for Mr. John Randolph and Mr. Giles to do this as to say it."

The trial formally opened on January 2, 1805, though the taking of testimony did not begin until the 9th of February. A contemporary description of the Senate chamber shows that the apostles of Republican simplicity, with the pomp of the Warren Hastings trial still fresh in mind, were not at all averse to making the scene as impressive as possible by the use of several different colors of cloth: "On the right and left of the President of the Senate, and in a right line with his chair, there are two rows of benches with desks in front, and the whole front and seats covered with crimson cloth. . . .

A temporary semi-circular gallery, which consists of three ranges of benches, is elevated on pillars and the whole front and seats thereof covered with green cloth. . . . In this gallery ladies are accommodated. . . . On the right and left hand of the President . . . are two boxes of two rows of seats . . . that facing the President's right is occupied by the managers . . . that on the other side of the bar for the accused and his counsel . . . these boxes are covered with blue cloth." To preside over this scene of somewhat dubious splendor came Aaron Burr, Vice-President of the United States, straight from the dueling ground at Weehawken.

The occasion brought forward one of the most extraordinary men of the day, Luther Martin, Chase's friend and the leader of his counsel. Born at New Brunswick, New Jersey, in 1744, Martin graduated from Princeton in 1766, the first of a class of thirty-five, among whom was Oliver Ellsworth. Five years later he began to practice law on the Eastern Shore of Maryland and in the adjoining counties of Virginia, where he won an immediate success, especially in criminal cases. At a single term of court, out of thirty defendants he procured the acquittal of twenty-nine, while the thirtieth, indicted for murder, was convicted of manslaughter. In 1805 Martin was the acknowledged head of the American Bar, but at the same time he was undoubtedly a drunkard and a spendthrift. With an income of $10,000 a year, he was always in need. His mediocre stature, thinning locks, and undistinguished features created an impression which was confirmed by his slovenly attire and ungrammatical speech, which seemed "shackled by a preternatural secretion of saliva." Here, indeed, for ugliness and caustic tongue was "the Thersites of the law." Yet once he was roused to action, his great resources made themselves apparent: a memory amounting to genius, a boyish delight in the rough-and-tumble of combat, a wealth of passion, kept in perfect curb till the enemy was already in rout before solid argument and then let loose with destroying effect. This child of nature was governed in his practice of the law less by retainers than by his personal loves and hatreds. Samuel Chase he loved and Thomas Jefferson he hated, and though his acquaintance with criminals had furnished him with a vituperative vocabulary of some amplitude, he considered no other damnation quite so scathing as to call a man "as great a scoundrel as Tom Jefferson."

The impeachers had no one whom they could pit against this "unprincipled and impudent Federalist bulldog," as Jefferson called him; and in other ways, too, from the first their lot was not easy. For one thing, they could not agree among themselves as to the proper scope of impeachment under the Constitution. Randolph, the leader of the House managers, and Campbell adhered in essence to Giles's theory. But Rodney and Nicholson, both much abler lawyers, openly disavowed such latitudinarian doctrine. In a general way, their view of the matter may be stated thus: Because judges of the United States are guaranteed continuance in office only during "good behavior," and because impeachment is the only method of removal recognized by the Constitution, the "high crimes and misdemeanors" for which impeachment is the constitutional resource must include all cases of willful misconduct in office, whether indictable or not. This seems sound theory and appears today to be established theory. But sound or not, the managers of the Republicans were not a unit in urging it, while their opponents put forward with confidence and unanimity the theory that "high crimes and misdemeanors" were always indictable offenses.

More calamitous still for the accusers of Chase

was the way in which, when the evidence began to
come in, the case against him started crumpling at
the corners.   Lewis, who had been Fries's attorney
and whose testimony they had chiefly relied upon
to prove the judge's unfairness on that occasion,
had not only acknowledged that his memory was
"not very tenacious" after so great a lapse of
time but had further admitted that he had really dropped the case because he thought it "more
likely that the President would pardon him [Fries]
after having been convicted without having counsel
th n if he had."   Similarly Hay, whose repeated
eff rts to bring the question of the constitutionality f the Sedition Act before the jury had caused
the rupture between court and counsel in Callender's case, owned that he had entertained "but
little hopes of doing Callender any good" but had
"wished to address the public on the constitutionality of the law."   Sensations multiplied on every
side.   A man named Heath testified that Chase
had told the marshal to strike all Democrats from
the panel which was to try Callender; whereupon
a second witness called to confirm this testimony
stated facts which showed the whole story to be a
deliberate fabrication.   The story that Chase had
attacked the Administration at Baltimore was also

substantially disproved by the managers' own witnesses. But the climax of absurdity was reached in the fifth and sixth articles of impeachment, which were based on the assumption that an act of Congress had required the procedure in Callender's case to be in accordance with the law of Virginia. In reply to this argument Chase's attorneys quickly pointed out that the statute relied upon applied only to actions between citizens of different States!

The final arguments began on the 20th of February. The first speech in behalf of Chase was delivered by Joseph Hopkinson, a young Philadelphia attorney, whose effort stirred the admiration of Federalists and Republicans alike. He dwelt upon "the infinite importance" of the implications of this case for the future of the Republic, contrasted the frivolity of the charges brought against Chase with the magnitude of the crimes of which Warren Hastings had been accused, and pointed out that, whereas in England only two judges had been impeached in half a century, in America, "boasting of its superior purity and virtue," seven judges had been prosecuted within two years. More loosely wrought, but not less effective was Martin's address, the superb climax of a remarkable forensic career! The accusation against Chase he reduced to a charge of indecorum, and he was ready to admit that the manner of his friend "bore a stronger resemblance to that of Lord Thurlow than of Lord Chesterfield," but, said he, our judges ought not to be "like the gods of Epicurus lolling upon their beds of down, equally careless whether the laws of their country are obeyed or violated, instead of *actively* discharging their duties."

The closing argument, which fell to the managers, was assigned to Randolph. It was an unmitigated disaster for the cause in behalf of which it was pronounced. "I feel perfectly inadequate to the task of closing this important debate on account of a severe indisposition which I labor under," were Randolph's opening words, but even this prefatory apology gave little warning of the distressing exhibition of incompetence which was to follow. "On the reopening of the court," records John Quincy Adams in his *Memoirs*, "he [Randolph] began a speech of about two hours and a half, with as little relation to the subject-matter as possible . . . without order, connection, or argument; consisting altogether of the most hackneyed commonplaces of popular declamation, mingled up with panegyrics and invectives upon persons, with a few well-expressed ideas, a few striking figures,

6

much distortion of face and contortion of body, tears, groans and sobs, with occasional pauses for recollection, and continual complaints of having lost his notes." So ended the ambition of John Randolph of Roanoke to prove himself another Burke!

But while their frontal assault on the reason of the court was thus breaking down, the impeachers, led by the President, were attempting a flank movement on its virtue. They especially distrusted the "steadiness" of certain New England and New York Senators and hoped to reach the hearts of these gentlemen through Aaron Burr, the Vice-President. Burr had heretofore found himself vested with the rôle of Lucifer in the Republican Paradise. Now he found himself suddenly basking in a perpetual sunburst of smiles both from the great central luminary, Jefferson, and his paler satellites, Madison and Gallatin. Invitations to the President's dinners were soon followed by more substantial bribes. Burr's step-son became judge of the Superior Court at New Orleans; his brother-in-law, secretary to the Louisiana Territory; his intimate friend Wilkinson, its military commandant. Then Giles, whose view of impeachment left him utterly shameless in the matter, drew up and circulated in the Senate itself a petition to the Governor of New Jersey asking him to quash the indictment for murder which the Bergen County grand jury had found against Burr as a result of the duel with Hamilton. At the same time, an act was passed giving the retiring Vice-President the franking privilege for life. In the debate Senator Wright of Maryland declared that dueling was justified by the example of David and Goliath and that the bill was opposed "only because *our* David had slain the Goliath of Federalism."

Whether Burr made any attempt to render the expected *quid pro quo* for these favors does not appear, but at least if he did, his efforts were fruitless. The vote on the impeachment of Chase was taken on the 1st of March, and the impeachers were crushingly defeated. On the first article they could muster only sixteen votes out of thirty-four; on the second, only ten; on the fifth, none; on the sixth, four. Even on the last article, where they made their best showing, they were still four votes short of the required constitutional majority. When the result of the last ballot was announced, Randolph rushed from the Senate chamber to the House to introduce a resolution proposing an amendment to the Constitution, requiring that judges of the United States "shall be removed by the President on joint address of both Houses of Congress." At the same time Nicholson moved an amendment providing legislative recall for Senators. Thus exasperation was vented and no harm done.

Meanwhile word had come from Philadelphia that the impeachment of the State Supreme Court judges had also failed. Here, even more impressively than in the case of Chase, had been illustrated that solidarity of Bench and Bar which has ever since been such an influential factor in American government. The Pennsylvania judge-breakers, failing to induce a single reputable member of the Philadelphia bar to aid them, had been obliged to go to Delaware, whence they procured Cæsar A. Rodney, one of the House managers against Chase. The two impeachments were thus closely connected and their results were similar. In the first place, it was determined that impeachment was likely to be, in the petulant language of Jefferson, "a farce" not soon to be used again for partisan purposes. In the second place, it was probable that henceforth, in the Commonwealths as well as in the National Government, political power would be exercised subject to constitutional restraints applied judicially. In the third place, however, the judges would henceforth have to be content with the possession of this magnificent prerogative and dispense with all judicial homilies on "manners and morals." It was a fair compromise and has on the whole proved a beneficial one.

CHAPTER IV

WHEN, on March 30, 1807, Colonel Aaron Burr, late Vice-President of the United States, was brought before Chief Justice Marshall in the Eagle Tavern at Richmond on the charge of treason, there began the greatest criminal trial in American history and one of the notable trials in the annals of the law.

"The Burr Conspiracy" still remains after a hundred years an unsolved enigma. Yet whether Burr actually planned treason against the United States in the year of grace 1806 is after all a question of somewhat restricted importance. The essential truth is that he was by nature an adventurer who, in the words of Hamilton, "believed all things possible to daring and energy," and that in 1806 he was a bankrupt and a social outcast to boot. Whether, therefore, his grandiose project of an empire on the ruins of Spanish dominion in Mexico involved also an effort to separate some part of the West from the Union is a question which, if it was ever definitely determined in Burr's own mind, was determined, we may be sure, quite independently of any moral or patriotic considerations.

Burr's activities after his term of public office ended in March, 1805, were devious, complicated, and purposely veiled, involving many men and spread over a large territory.[1] Near Marietta on an island in the Ohio River, Burr came upon Harman Blennerhassett, a genial Irishman living in a luxurious and hospitable mansion which was making a heavy drain upon his already diminished resources. Here Burr, by his charm of manner and engaging conversation, soon won from the simple Irishman his heart and his remaining funds. He also made the island both a convenient rendezvous for his adherents in his ambitious schemes and a starting point for his own extended expeditions, which took him during the latter part of this year to Natchez, Nashville, St. Louis, Vincennes, Cincinnati, and Philadelphia, and back to Washington.

In the summer of 1806 Burr turned westward

[1] An account of the Burr conspiracy will be found in *Jefferson and his Colleagues*, by Allen Johnson (in *The Chronicles of America*).

a second time and with the assistance of Blennerhassett he began military preparations on the
latter's island for a mysterious expedition. On
the 29th of July, Burr had dispatched a letter in
cipher to Wilkinson, his most important confed-
erate. The precise terms of this document we
shall never know, but apparently it contained the
most amazing claims of the successful maturing of
Burr's scheme: "funds had been obtained," "English naval protection had been secured," "from
five hundred to a thousand men" would be on
the move down the Mississippi by the middle of
November. Unfortunately for Burr, however, Wilkinson was far too expert in the usages of ini-
quity to be taken in by such audacious lying as
this. He guessed that the enterprise was on the
verge of collapse and forthwith made up his mind
to abandon it.

Meanwhile exaggerated accounts of the size of
Burr's following were filtering to Washington, together with circumstantial rumors of the disloy-
alty of his designs. Yet for weeks Jefferson did
nothing, until late in November his alarm was
aroused by a letter from Wilkinson, dated the
21st of October. On the 27th of November the
President issued a proclamation calling upon all

good citizens to seize "sundry persons" who were charged with setting on foot a military expedition against Spain. Already Burr, realizing that the West was not so hot for disunion as perhaps he had supposed it to be, began to represent his project as a peaceful emigration to the Washita, a precaution which, however, came too late to allay the rising excitement of the people. Fearing the seizure of their equipment, thirty or forty of Burr's followers under the leadership of Blennerhassett left the island in four or five flatboats for New Orleans, on the night of the 10th of December, and a few days later were joined by Burr himself at the mouth of the Cumberland. When the little expedition paused near Natchez, on the 10th of January, Burr was confronted with a newspaper containing a transcription of his fatal letter to Wilkinson. A week later, learning that his former ally, Wilkinson, had now established a reign of terror at New Orleans directed against his followers, and feeling no desire to test the tender mercies of a court-martial presided over by his former associate, Burr surrendered himself into the custody of the acting Governor of Mississippi Territory. But the refusal of the territorial grand jury to indict him suggested the hope that he might

still escape from the reach of the law. He therefore plunged into the wilderness, headed for the
Spanish border, and had all but reached his des-
tination when he was recognized and recaptured at
Wakefield, Alabama.

Owing to the peculiar and complicated circumstances which led up to it, Burr's case was from the
outset imbued with factional and partisan politics
of the most extreme kind. While the conspiracy
was at its height, Jefferson, though emphatically
warned, had refused to lend it any credence whatever; but when the danger was well over he had
thrown the whole country into a panic, and had
even asked Congress to suspend the writ of habeas
corpus. The Federalists and the President's enemies within his own party, headed by the re-
doubtable Randolph, were instantly alert to the
opportunity which Jefferson's inexplicable conduct
afforded them. "The mountain had labored and
brought forth a mouse," quoted the supercilious;
the executive dragnet had descended to envelop
the monster which was ready to split the Union
or at least to embroil its relations with a friendly
power, and had brought up — a few peaceful agri-
culturists! Nor was this the worst of the matter,
contended these critics of the Administration, for

the real source of the peril had been the President's own action in assigning the command at New Orleans to Wilkinson, a pensioner of Spain, a villain "from the bark to the very core." Yet so far was the President from admitting this error that he now attributed the salvation of the country to "the soldier's honor" and "the citizen's fidelity" of this same Wilkinson. Surely, then, the real defendants before the bar of opinion were Thomas Jefferson and his precious ally James Wilkinson, not their harried and unfortunate victim, Aaron Burr!

The proceedings against Burr occupied altogether some seven months, during which the sleepy little town of Richmond became the cynosure of all eyes. So famous was the case that it brought thither of necessity or out of curiosity men of every rank and grade of life, of every species of renown. The prosecution was in charge of the United States District Attorney, George Hay — serious, humorless, faithful to Jefferson's interests, and absolutely devoid of the personal authority demanded by so grave a cause. He was assisted by William Wirt, already a brilliant lawyer and possessed of a dazzling elocution, but sadly lacking in the majesty of years. At the head and forefront of the defense stood Burr himself, an unerring legal tactician, deciding every move of the great game, the stake of which for him was life itself. About him were gathered the ablest members of the Richmond bar: John Wickham, witty and ingenious, Edmund Randolph, ponderous and pontifical, Benjamin Botts, learned and sarcastic, while from Baltimore came Luther Martin to aid his "highly respected friend," to keep the political pot boiling, and eventually to fall desperately in love with Burr's daughter, the beautiful Theodosia. Among the 140 witnesses there were also some notable figures: William Eaton, the hero of Derne, whom Burr's codefendant, Blennerhassett, describes for us as "strutting about the streets under a tremendous hat, with a Turkish sash over colored clothes," and offering up, with his frequent libations in the taverns, "the copious effusions of his sorrows"; Commodore Truxton, the gallant commander of the *Constellation;* General Andrew Jackson, future President of the United States, but now a vehement declaimer of Burr's innocence — out of abundant caution for his own reputation, it may be surmised; Erick Bollmann, once a participant in the effort to release Lafayette from Olmutz and himself just now released from durance vile on a writ of habeas corpus from the Supreme Court; Samuel Swartwout, another tool of Burr's, reserved by the same beneficent writ for a career of political roguery which was to culminate in his swindling the Government out of a million and a quarter dollars; and finally the bibulous and traitorous Wilkinson, "whose head" as he himself owned, "might err," but "whose heart could not deceive." Traveling by packet from New Orleans, this essential witness was heralded by the impatient prosecution, till at last he burst upon the stage with all the éclat of the hero in a melodrama — only to retire baffled and perplexed, his villainy guessed by his own partisans.

By the Constitution treason against the United States consists "only in levying war against them, or in adhering to their enemies, giving them aid and comfort," and no person may be convicted of it "unless on the testimony of two witnesses to the same overt act, or on confession in open court." The motion to commit Burr for treason thus raised at the outset the question whether in this case an "overt act" existed. Marshall, who held that no evidence had been shown to this effect, denied the motion, but consented to commit the prisoner on the lesser charge that he had attempted a military expedition against Spain. As this was a bailable offense, however, Burr was soon at liberty once more.

Nor was this the only respect in which the preliminary proceedings sounded a note of antagonism between the Chief Justice and the Administration which was to recur again and yet again in the months following. Only a few weeks earlier at Washington, Marshall had, though with some apparent reluctance, ordered the release of Bollmann and Swartwout, two of Burr's tools, from the custody of the Federal authorities. Alluding in his present opinion to his reason for his earlier action, he wrote: "More than five weeks have elapsed since the opinion of the Supreme Court has declared the necessity of proving the fact, if it exists. Why is it not proved? To the executive government is entrusted the important power of prosecuting those whose crimes may disturb the public repose or endanger its safety. It would be easy, in much less time than has intervened since Colonel Burr has been alleged to have assembled his troops, to procure affidavits establishing the fact."

This sharp criticism brought an equally sharp retort from Jefferson, to which was added a threat.

In a private letter of the 20th of April, the President said: "In what terms of decency can we speak of this? As if an express could go to Natchez or the mouth of the Cumberland and return in five weeks, to do which has never taken less than twelve! . . . But all the principles of law are to be perverted which would bear on the favorite offenders who endeavor to overturn this odious republic! . . . All this, however, will work well. The nation will judge both the offender and judges for themselves. . . . They will see then and amend the error in our Constitution which makes any branch independent of the nation. . . . If their [the judges] protection of Burr produces this amendment, it will do more good than his condemnation would have done." Already the case had taken on the color of a fresh contest between the President and the Chief Justice.

On the 22d of May the United States Court for the Fifth Circuit and the Virginia District formally convened, with Marshall presiding and Judge Griffin at his side. On the same day the grand jury was sworn, with John Randolph as foreman, and presently began taking testimony. Unluckily for the prosecution, the proceedings now awaited the arrival of Wilkinson and the delay was turned to skillful use by the defense to embroil further the relations between the Chief Justice and the President. With this end in view, Burr moved on the 9th of June that a *subpœna duces tecum* issue to Jefferson requiring him to produce certain papers, including the famous cipher letter to Wilkinson. The main question involved, of course, was that of the right of the Court under any circumstances to issue a subpœna to the President, but the abstract issue soon became involved with a much more irritating personal one. "This," said Luther Martin, who now found himself in his element, "this is a peculiar case, sir. The President has undertaken to prejudge my client by declaring that 'of his guilt there is no doubt.' He has assumed to himself the knowledge of the Supreme Being himself and pretended to search the heart of my highly respected friend. He has proclaimed him a traitor in the face of the country which has rewarded him. He has let slip the dogs of war, the hell-hounds of persecution, to hunt down my friend. And would this President of the United States, who has raised all this absurd clamor, pretend to keep back the papers which are wanted for this trial, where life itself is at stake?"

Wirt's answer to Martin was also a rebuke to the

Court. "Do they [the defense] flatter themselves," he asked, "that this court feel political prejudices which will supply the place of argument and innocence on the part of the prisoner? Their conduct amounts to an insinuation of the sort. But I do not believe it. . . . Sir, no man, foreigner or citizen, who hears this language addressed to the court, and received with all the complacency at least which silence can imply, can make any inference from it very honorable to the court." These words touched Marshall's conscience, as well they might. At the close of the day he asked counsel henceforth to "confine themselves to the point really before the court" — a request which, however, was by no means invariably observed through the following days.

A day or two later Marshall ruled that the subpœna should issue, holding that neither the personal nor the official character of the President exempted him from the operation of that constitutional clause which guarantees accused persons "compulsory process for obtaining witnesses" in their behalf. The demand made upon the President, said the Chief Justice, by his official duties is not an unremitting one, and, "if it should exist at the time when his attendance on a court is required, it would be sworn on the return of the subpœna and would rather constitute a reason for not obeying the process of the court than a reason against its being issued." Jefferson, however, neither obeyed the writ nor swore anything on its return, though he forwarded some of the papers required to Hay, the district attorney, to be used as the latter might deem best. The President's argument was grounded on the mutual independence of the three departments of Government; and he asked whether the independence of the Executive could long survive "if the smaller courts could bandy him from pillar to post, keep him constantly trudging from North to South and East to West, and withdraw him entirely from his executive duties?" The President had the best of the encounter on all scores. Not only had Marshall forgotten for the nonce the doctrine he himself had stated in Marbury *vs.* Madison regarding the constitutional discretion of the Executive, but what was worse still, he had forgotten his own discretion on that occasion. He had fully earned his rebuff, but that fact did not appreciably sweeten it.

On the 24th of June the grand jury reported two indictments against Burr, one for treason and the other for misdemeanor. The former charged that

Burr, moved thereto "by the instigation of the devil," had on the 10th of December previous levied war against the United States at Blenner-hassett's island, in the county of Wood, of the District of Virginia, and had on the day following, at the same place, set in motion a warlike array against the city of New Orleans. The latter charged that a further purpose of this same warlike array was an invasion of Mexico. Treason not being a bailable offense, Burr had now to go to jail, but, as the city jail was alleged to be unhealthful, the Court allowed him to be removed to quarters which had been proffered by the Governor of the State in the penitentiary just outside the city. Burr's situation here, writes his biographer, "was extremely agreeable. He had a suite of rooms in the third story, extending one hundred feet, where he was allowed to see his friends without the presence of a witness. His rooms were so thronged with visitors at times as to present the appearance of a levee. Servants were continually arriving with messages, notes, and inquiries, bringing oranges, lemons, pineapples, raspberries, apricots, cream, butter, ice, and other articles — presents from the ladies of the city. In expectation of his daughter's arrival, some of his friends in town provided a house for her accommodation. The jailer, too, was all civility."[1] Little wonder that such goings-on are said to have "filled the measure of Jefferson's disgust."

The trial itself opened on Monday, the 3d of August. The first business in hand was to get a jury which would answer to the constitutional requirement of impartiality — a task which it was soon discovered was likely to prove a difficult one. The original panel of forty-eight men contained only four who had not expressed opinions unfavorable to the prisoner, and of these four all but one admitted some degree of prejudice against him. These four were nevertheless accepted as jurors. A second panel was then summoned which was even more unpromising in its make-up, and Burr's counsel began hinting that the trial would have to be quashed, when Burr himself arose and offered to select eight out of the whole *venire* to add to the four previously chosen. The offer was accepted, and notwithstanding that several of the jurors thus obtained had publicly declared opinions hostile to the accused, the jury was sworn in on the 17th of August.

[1] Parton's *Life and Times of Aaron Burr* (13th Edition, N. Y., 1860), p. 479.

At first glance Burr's concession in the selecting of a jury seems extraordinary. But then, why should one so confident of being able to demonstrate his innocence fear prejudice which rested on no firmer basis than ignorance of the facts? This reflection, however, probably played small part in Burr's calculations, for already he knew that if the contemplated strategy of his counsel prevailed the case would never come before the jury.

The first witness called by the prosecution was Eaton, who was prepared to recount the substance of numerous conversations he had held with Burr in Washington in the winter of 1805–6, in which Burr had gradually unveiled to him the treasonable character of his project. No sooner, however, was Eaton sworn than the defense entered the objection that his testimony was not yet relevant, contending that in a prosecution for treason the great material fact on which the merits of the entire controversy pivots was the overt act, which must be *"an open act of war"*; just as in a murder trial the fact of the killing, the *corpus delicti*, must be proved before any other testimony was relevant, so in the pending prosecution, said they, no testimony was admissible until the overt act had been shown in the manner required by the Constitution.

The task of answering this argument fell to Wirt, who argued, and apparently with justice, that the prosecution was free to introduce its evidence in any order it saw fit, provided only that the evidence was relevant to the issue raised by the indictment, and that if an overt act was proved "in the course of the whole evidence," that would be sufficient. The day following the Court read an opinion which is a model of ambiguous and equivocal statement, but the purport was fairly clear: for the moment the Court would not interfere, and the prosecution was free to proceed as it thought best, with the warning that the Damocles sword of "irrelevancy" was suspended over its head by the barest thread and might fall at any moment.

For the next two days the legal battle was kept in abeyance while the taking of testimony went forward. Eaton was followed on the stand by Commodore Truxton, who stated that in conversation with him Burr had seemed to be aiming only at an expedition against Mexico. Then came General Morgan and his two sons, who asserted their belief in the treasonable character of Burr's designs.

Finally a series of witnesses, the majority of them servants of Blennerhassett, testified that on the evening of December 10, 1806, Burr's forces had assembled on the island.

This line of testimony concluded, the prosecution next indicated its intention of introducing evidence to show Burr's connection with the assemblage on the island, when the defense sprang the *coup* it had been maturing from the outset. Pointing out the notorious fact that on the night of the 10th of December Burr had not been present at the island but had been two hundred miles away in Kentucky, they contended that, under the Constitution, the assemblage on Blennerhassett's island could not be regarded as his act, even granting that he had advised it, for, said they, advising war is one thing but levying it is quite another. If this interpretation was correct, then no overt act of levying war, either within the jurisdiction of the Court or stated in the indictment, had been, or could be, shown against Burr. Hence the taking of evidence — if not the cause itself, indeed — should be discontinued.

The legal question raised by this argument was the comparatively simple one whether the constitutional provision regarding treason was to be interpreted in the light of the Common Law doctrine that "in treason all are principals." For if it were to be so interpreted and if Burr's connection with the general conspiracy culminating in the assemblage was demonstrable by any sort of legal evidence, then the assemblage was his act, his overt act, proved moreover by thrice the two witnesses constitutionally required! Again it fell to Wirt to represent the prosecution, and he discharged his task most brilliantly. He showed beyond peradventure that the Common Law doctrine was grounded upon unshakable authority; that, considering the fact that the entire phraseology of the constitutional clause regarding treason comes from an English statute of Edward III's time, it was reasonable, if not indispensable, to construe it in the light of the Common Law; and that, certainly as to a procurer of treason, such as Burr was charged with being, the Common Law doctrine was the only just doctrine, being merely a reaffirmation of the even more ancient principle that "what one does through another, he does himself."

In elaboration of this last point Wirt launched forth upon that famous passage in which he contrasted Burr and the pathetic victim of his conspiracy:

Who [he asked] is Blennerhassett? A native of Ireland, a man of letters, who fled from the storms of his own country to find quiet in ours. . . . Possessing himself of a beautiful island in the Ohio he rears upon it a palace and decorates it with every romantic embellishment of fancy. [Then] in the midst of all this peace, this innocent simplicity, this pure banquet of the heart, the destroyer comes . . . to change this paradise into a hell. . . . By degrees he infuses [into the heart of Blennerhassett] the poison of his own ambition. . . . In a short time the whole man is changed, and every object of his former delight is relinquished. . . . His books are abandoned. . . . His enchanted island is destined soon to relapse into a wilderness; and in a few months we find the beautiful and tender partner of his bosom, whom he lately 'permitted not the winds of summer to visit too roughly,' we find her shivering at midnight on the winter banks of the Ohio and mingling her tears with the torrents that froze as they fell. Yet this unfortunate man, thus ruined, and undone and made to play a subordinate part in this grand drama of guilt and treason, this man is to be called the principal offender, while he by whom he was thus plunged in misery is comparatively innocent, a mere accessory! Is this reason? Is it law? Is it humanity? Sir, neither the human heart nor the human understanding will bear a perversion so monstrous and absurd!

But there was one human heart, one human understanding — and that, in ordinary circumstances, a very good one — which was quite willing to shoulder just such a monstrous perversion, or at least its equivalent, and that heart was John Marshall's. The discussion of the motion to arrest the evidence continued ten days, most of the time being occupied by Burr's attorneys.[1] Finally, on the last day of the month, the Chief Justice handed down an opinion accepting practically the whole contention of Burr's attorneys, but offering a totally new set of reasons for it. On the main question at issue, namely, whether under the Constitution all involved in a treasonable enterprise are principals, Marshall pretended not to pass; but in fact he rejected the essential feature of the Common Law doctrine, namely, the necessary legal presence at the scene of action of all parties to the conspiracy. The crux of his argument he embodied in the following statement: "If in one case the

[1] A recurrent feature of their arguments was a denunciation of "constructive treason." But this was mere declamation. Nobody was charging Burr with any sort of treason except that which is specifically defined by the Constitution itself, namely, the levying of war against the United States. The only question at issue was as to the method of proof by which this crime may be validly established in the case of one accused of procuring treason. There was also much talk about the danger and injustice of dragging a man from one end of the country to stand trial for an act committed at the other end of it. The answer was that, if the man himself procured the act or joined others in bringing it about, he ought to stand trial where the act occurred. This same "injustice" may happen today in the case of murder!

presence of the individual make the guilt of the
[treasonable] assemblage *his* guilt, and in the other
case, the procurement by the individual make the
guilt of the [treasonable] assemblage, his guilt, then
presence and procurement are equally component
parts of the overt act, and equally require two
witnesses." Unfortunately for this argument, the
Constitution does not require that the "component
parts" of the overt act be proved by two witnesses,
but only that the overt act — the *corpus delicti* —
be so proved; and for the simple reason that, when
by further evidence any particular individual is
connected with the treasonable combination which
brought about the overt act, that act, assuming
the Common Law doctrine, becomes his act, and
he is accordingly responsible for it at the place
where it occurred. Burr's attorneys admitted this
contention unreservedly. Indeed, that was precisely the reason why they had opposed the Common Law doctrine.

Marshall's effort to steer between this doctrine
and its obvious consequences for the case before
him placed him, therefore, in the curious position
of demanding that two overt acts be proved each by
two witnesses. But if two, why not twenty? For
it must often happen that the traitor's connection

with the overt act is demonstrable not by a single act but a series of acts. Furthermore, in the case of procurers of treason, this connection will ordinarily not appear in overt acts at all but, as in Burr's own case, will be covert. Can it be, then, that the Constitution is chargeable with the absurdity of regarding the procurers of treason as traitors and yet of making their conviction impossible? The fact of the matter was that six months earlier, before his attitude toward Burr's doings had begun to take color from his hatred and distrust of Jefferson, Marshall had entertained no doubt that the Common Law doctrine underlay the constitutional definition of treason. Speaking for the Supreme Court in the case of Bollmann and Swartwout, he had said: "It is not the intention of the Court to say that no individual can be guilty of this crime who has not appeared in arms against his country; on the contrary, if war be actually levied, that is, if a body of men be actually assembled for the purpose of effecting by force a treasonable purpose, all those who perform any part however minute, or however remote from the scene of action, and who are actually leagued in the general conspiracy, are to be considered traitors." Marshall's effort to square this previous opinion with his later position was as unconvincing as it was labored.[1]

Burr's attorneys were more prudent: they dismissed Marshall's earlier words outright as *obiter dicta* — and erroneous at that! Nevertheless when, thirty years later, Story, Marshall's friend and pupil, was in search of the best judicial definition of treason within the meaning of the Constitution, he selected this sentence from the case of Bollmann and Swartwout and passed by the elaborate opinion in Burr's case in significant silence. But reputation is a great magician in transmuting heresy into accepted teaching. Posthumously Marshall's opinion has attained a rank and authority with the legal profession that it never enjoyed in his own time. Regarding it, therefore, as today established doctrine, we may say that it has quite reversed the relative importance of conspiracy and overt act where the treason is by levying

[1] The way in which Marshall proceeded to do this was to treat the phrase "perform a part" as demanding "a levying of war" on the part of the performer. (Robertson, *Reports*, vol. II, p. 438.) But this explanation will not hold water. For what then becomes of the phrase "scene of action" in the passage just quoted? What is the difference between the part to be performed "however minute," and the "action" from which the performer may be "however remote"? It is perfectly evident that the "action" referred to is the assemblage which is regarded as the overt act of war, and that the "part however minute" is something very different.

war. At the Common Law, and in the view of the framers of the Constitution, the importance of the overt act of war was to make the conspiracy visible, to put its existence beyond surmise. By Marshall's view each traitor is chargeable only with his own overt acts, and the conspiracy is of importance merely as showing the intention of such acts. And from this it results logically, as Marshall saw, though he did not venture to say so explicitly, that the procurer of treason is not a traitor unless he has also participated personally in an overt act of war. As Wirt very justifiably contended, such a result is "monstrous," and, what is more, it has not been possible to adhere to it in practice. In recent legislation necessitated by the Great War, Congress has restored the old Common Law view of treason but has avoided the constitutional difficulty by labeling the offense "Espionage." Indeed, the Espionage Act of June 15, 1917, scraps Marshall's opinion pretty completely.[1]

On the day following the reading of Marshall's

---

[1] See especially Title I, Section 4, of the Act. For evidence of the modern standing of Marshall's opinion, see the chorus of approval sounded by the legal fraternity in Dillon's three volumes. In support of the Common Law doctrine, see the authorities cited in 27 *Yale Law Journal*, p. 342 and footnotes; the chapter on Treason in Simon Greenleaf's well-known *Treatise on the Law of Evidence;* United States *vs.* Mitchell, 2 Dallas, 348; and Druecker *vs.* Salomon, 21 Wis., 621.

opinion, the prosecution, unable to produce two witnesses who had actually *seen* Burr procure the assemblage on the island, abandoned the case to the jury. Shortly thereafter the following verdict was returned: "We of the jury say that Aaron Burr is not proved to be guilty under this indictment by any evidence submitted to us. We therefore find him not guilty." At the order of the Chief Justice this Scotch verdict was entered on the records of the court as a simple Not Guilty.

Marshall's conduct of Burr's trial for treason is the one serious blemish in his judicial record, but for all that it was not without a measure of extenuation. The President, too, had behaved deplorably and, feeling himself on the defensive, had pressed matters with most unseemly zeal, so that the charge of political persecution raised by Burr's attorneys was, to say the least, not groundless. Furthermore, in opposing the President in this matter, Marshall had shown his usual political sagacity. Had Burr been convicted, the advantage must all have gone to the Administration. The only possible credit the Chief Justice could extract from the case would be from assuming that lofty tone of calm, unmoved impartiality of which Marshall was such a master — and never more than on this occasion — and from setting himself sternly against popular hysteria. The words with which his opinion closes have been often quoted:

Much has been said in the course of the argument on points on which the Court feels no inclination to comment particularly, but which may, perhaps not improperly receive some notice.

That this Court dare not usurp power is most true.

That this Court dare not shrink from its duty is not less true.

No man is desirous of placing himself in a disagreeable situation. No man is desirous of becoming the popular subject of calumny. No man, might he let the bitter cup pass from him without self-reproach, would drain it to the bottom. But if he have no choice in the case, if there be no alternative presented to him but a dereliction of duty or the opprobrium of those who are denominated the world, he merits the contempt as well as the indignation of his country who can hesitate which to embrace.

One could not require a better illustration of that faculty of "apparently deep self-conviction" which Wirt had noted in the Chief Justice.

Finally, it must be owned that Burr's case offered Marshall a tempting opportunity to try out the devotion of Republicans to that ideal of judicial deportment which had led them so vehemently to criticize Justice Chase and to charge him with being "oppressive," with refusing to give counsel for defense an opportunity to be heard, with transgressing the state law of procedure, with showing too great liking for Common Law ideas of sedition, with setting up the President as a sort of monarch beyond the reach of judicial process. Marshall's conduct of Burr's trial now exactly reversed every one of these grounds of complaint. Whether he intended it or not, it was a neat turning of the tables.

But Jefferson, who was at once both the most theoretical and the least logical of men, was of course hardly prepared to see matters in that light. As soon as the news reached him of Burr's acquittal, he ordered Hay to press the indictment for misdemeanor — not for the purpose of convicting Burr, but of getting the evidence down in a form in which it should be available for impeachment proceedings against Marshall. For some weeks longer, therefore, the Chief Justice sat listening to evidence which was to be used against himself. But the impeachment never came, for a chain is only as strong as its weakest link, and the weakest link in the combination against the Chief Justice was a very fragile one indeed — the iniquitous Wilkinson. Even the faithful and melancholy Hay finally abandoned him. "The declaration which I made in court in his favor some time ago," he wrote the President, "was precipitate. . . . My confidence in him is destroyed. . . . I am sorry for it, on his account, on the public account, and because you have expressed opinions in his favor." It was obviously impossible to impeach the Chief Justice for having prevented the hanging of Aaron Burr on the testimony of such a miscreant.

Though the years immediately following the Burr trial were not a time of conspicuous activity for Marshall, they paved the way in more than one direction for his later achievement. Jefferson's retirement from the Presidency at last relieved the Chief Justice from the warping influence of a hateful personal contest and from anxiety for his official security. Jefferson's successors were men more willing to identify the cause of the Federal Judiciary with that of national unity. Better still, the War of 1812 brought about the demise of the Federalist party and thus cleared the Court of every suspicion of partisan bias. Henceforth the great political issue was the general one of the nature of the Union and the Constitution, a field in which Marshall's talent for debate made him master.

In the meantime the Court was acquiring that personnel which it was to retain almost intact for nearly twenty years; and, although the new recruits came from the ranks of his former party foes, Marshall had little trouble in bringing their views into general conformity with his own constitutional creed.   Nor was his triumph an exclusively personal one.   He was aided in very large measure by the fact that the war had brought particularism temporarily into discredit in all sections of the country.   Of Marshall's associates in 1812, Justice Washington alone had come to the bench earlier, yet he was content to speak through the mouth of his illustrious colleague, save on the notable occasion when he led the only revolt of a majority of the Court from the Chief Justice's leadership in the field of Constitutional Law.[1]   Johnson of South Carolina, a man of no little personal vanity, affected a greater independence, for which he was on one occasion warmly congratulated by Jefferson; yet even his separate opinions, though they sometimes challenge Marshall's more sweeping premises and bolder method of reasoning, are after all mostly concurring ones.   Marshall's really invaluable

[1] This was in the case of Ogden *vs.* Saunders, 12 Wheaton, 213 (1827).

aid among his associates was Joseph Story, who in 1811, at the age of thirty-two, was appointed by Madison in succession to Cushing. Still immature, enthusiastically willing to learn, warmly affectionate, and with his views on constitutional issues as yet unformed, Story fell at once under the spell of Marshall's equally gentle but vastly more resolute personality; and the result was one of the most fruitful friendships of our history. Marshall's "original bias," to quote Story's own words, "as well as the choice of his mind, was to general principles and comprehensive views, rather than to technical or recondite learning." Story's own bias, which was supported by his prodigious industry, was just the reverse. The two men thus supplemented each other admirably. A tradition of some venerability represents Story as having said that Marshall was wont to remark: "Now Story, that is the law; you find the precedents for it." Whether true or not, the tale at least illustrates the truth. Marshall owed to counsel a somewhat similar debt in the way of leading up to his decisions, for, as Story points out, "he was solicitous to hear arguments and not to decide cases without them, nor did any judge ever profit more by them." But in the field of Constitutional Law, at

least, Marshall used counsel's argument not so much to indicate what his own judicial goal ought to be as to discover the best route thereto — often, indeed, through the welcome stimulus which a clash of views gave to his reasoning powers.

Though the wealth of available legal talent at this period was impressively illustrated in connection both with Chase's impeachment and with Burr's trial, yet on neither of these occasions appeared William Pinkney of Maryland, the attorney to whom Marshall acknowledged his greatest indebtedness, and who was universally acknowledged to be the leader of the American Bar from 1810 until his death twelve years later. Besides being a great lawyer, Pinkney was also a notable personality, as George Ticknor's sketch of him as he appeared before the Supreme Court in 1815 goes to prove:

You must imagine, if you can, a man formed on nature's most liberal scale, who at the age of 50 is possessed with the ambition of being a pretty fellow, wears corsets to diminish his bulk, uses cosmetics, as he told Mrs. Gore, to smooth and soften a skin growing somewhat wrinkled and rigid with age, dresses in a style which would be thought foppish in a much younger man. You must imagine such a man standing before the gravest tribunal in the land, and engaged in causes of the deepest moment; but still apparently thinking how he can declaim like a practised rhetorician in the London Cockpit, which he used to frequent. Yet you must, at the same time, imagine his declamation to be chaste and precise in its language and cogent, logical and learned in its argument, free from the artifice and affectation of his manner, and in short, opposite to what you might fairly have expected from his first appearance and tones. And when you have compounded these inconsistencies in your imagination, and united qualities which on common occasions nature seems to hold asunder, you will, perhaps, begin to form some idea of what Mr. Pinkney is.

Such was the man whom Marshall, Story, and Taney all considered the greatest lawyer who had ever appeared before the Supreme Court.

At the close of the War of 1812, Marshall, though he had decided many important questions of International Law,[1] nevertheless found himself only at the threshold of his real fame. Yet even thus early he had indicated his point of view. Thus in the case of the United States *vs.* Peters,[2] which was decided in 1809, the question before the Court was whether a mandamus should issue to the United States District Judge of Pennsylvania ordering him to enforce, in the face of the opposition of

[1] Two famous decisions of Marshall's in this field are those in the Schooner *Exchange vs.* McFaddon *et al*, 7 Cranch, 116, and the case of the *Nereide,* 9 *ib.*, 388.

[2] 5 Cranch, 136.

the state Government, a decision handed down in a prize case more than thirty years before by the old Committee of Appeals of the Continental Congress. Marshall answered the question affirmatively, saying: "If the legislatures of the several states may, at will, annul the judgments of the courts of the United States and destroy the rights acquired under those judgments, the Constitution itself becomes a solemn mockery, and the nation is deprived of the means of enforcing its laws by the instrumentality of its own tribunals."

Marshall's decision evoked a warm protest from the Pennsylvania Legislature and led to a proposal of amendment to the Constitution providing "an impartial tribunal" between the General Government and the States; and these expressions of dissent in turn brought the Virginia Assembly to the defense of the Supreme Court.

The commission to whom was referred the communication of the governor of Pennsylvania [reads the Virginia document] . . . are of the opinion that a tribunal is already provided by the Constitution of the United States, *to wit;* the Supreme Court, more eminently qualified from their habits and duties, from the mode of their selection, and from the tenure of their offices, to decide the disputes aforesaid in an enlightened and impartial manner than any other tribunal which could be created.

The members of the Supreme Court are selected from those in the United States who are most celebrated for virtue and legal learning. . . . The duties they have to perform lead them necessarily to the most enlarged and accurate acquaintance with the jurisdiction of the federal and several State courts together, and with the admirable symmetry of our government. The tenure of their offices enables them to pronounce the sound and correct opinions they have formed, without fear, favor or partiality.

Was it coincidence or something more that during Marshall's incumbency Virginia paid her one and only tribute to the impartiality of the Supreme Court while Burr's acquittal was still vivid in the minds of all? Or was it due to the fact that "the Great Lama of the Little Mountain" — to use Marshall's disrespectful appellation for Jefferson — had not yet converted the Virginia Court of Appeals into the angry oracle of his own unrelenting hatred of the Chief Justice? Whatever the reason, within five years Virginia's attitude had again shifted, and she had become once more what she had been in 1798–99, the rallying point of the forces of Confederation and State Rights.

CHAPTER V

THE TENETS OF NATIONALISM

"JOHN MARSHALL stands in history as one of that small group of men who have founded States. He was a nation-maker, a state-builder. His monument is in the history of the United States and his name is written upon the Constitution of his country." So spoke Senator Lodge, on John Marshall Day, February 4, 1901. "I should feel a . . . doubt," declared Justice Holmes on the same occasion, "whether, after Hamilton and the Constitution itself, Marshall's work proved more than a strong intellect, a good style, personal ascendancy in his court, courage, justice, and the convictions of his party." Both these divergent estimates of the great Chief Justice have their value. It is well to be reminded that Marshall's task lay within the four corners of the Constitution, whose purposes he did not originate, especially since no one would have been quicker than himself to disown praise implying anything different. None the less it was no ordinary skill and courage which, assisted by great office, gave enduring definition to the purposes of the Constitution at the very time when the whole trend of public opinion was setting in most strongly against them. It must not be forgotten that Hamilton, whose name Justice Holmes invokes in his somewhat too grudging encomium of Marshall, had pronounced the Constitution "a frail and worthless fabric."

Marshall's own outlook upon his task sprang in great part from a profound conviction of calling. He was thoroughly persuaded that he knew the intentions of the framers of the Constitution — the intentions which had been wrought into the instrument itself — and he was equally determined that these intentions should prevail. For this reason he refused to regard his office merely as a judicial tribunal; it was a platform from which to promulgate sound constitutional principles, the very cathedra indeed of constitutional orthodoxy. Not one of the cases which elicited his great opinions but might easily have been decided on comparatively narrow grounds in precisely the same way in which he decided it on broad, general principles, but with the probable result that it would never again have been heard of outside the law courts. To take a timid or obscure way to a merely tentative goal would have been at variance equally with Marshall's belief in his mission and with his instincts as a great debater.   Hence he forged his weapon — the *obiter dictum* — by whose broad strokes was hewn the highroad of a national destiny.

Marshall's task naturally was not performed *in vacuo:* he owed much to the preconceptions of his contemporaries. His invariable quest, as students of his opinions are soon aware, was for the axiomatic, for absolute principles, and in this inquiry he met the intellectual demands of a period whose first minds still owned the sway of the syllogism and still loved what Bacon called the "spacious liberty of generalities."   In Marshall's method — as in the older syllogistic logic, whose phraseology begins to sound somewhat strange to twentieth century ears — the essential operation consisted in eliminating the "accidental" or "irrelevant" elements from the "significant" facts of a case, and then recognizing that this particular case had been foreseen and provided for in a general rule of law.   Proceeding in this way Marshall was able to build up a body of thought the internal consistency of which, even when it did not convince, yet baffled the only sort of criticism which contemporaries were disposed to apply. Listen, for instance, to the despairing cry of John Randolph of Roanoke: "All wrong," said he of one of Marshall's opinions, "all wrong, but no man in the United States can tell why or wherein."

Marshall found his first opportunity to elaborate the tenets of his nationalistic creed in the case of M'Culloch *vs.* Maryland, which was decided at the same term with the Dartmouth College case and that of Sturges *vs.* Crowinshield — the greatest six weeks in the history of the Court. The question immediately involved was whether the State of Maryland had the right to tax the notes issued by the branch which the Bank of the United States had recently established at Baltimore. But this question raised the further one whether the United States had in the first place the right to charter the Bank and to authorize it to establish branches within the States. The outcome turned on the interpretation to be given the "necessary and proper" clause of the Constitution.

The last two questions were in 1819 by no means novel. In the *Federalist* itself Hamilton had boldly asked, "Who is to judge of the necessity and propriety of the laws to be passed for executing the powers of the Union?" and had announced that "the National Government, like every other, must judge in the first instance, of the proper exercise of its powers, and its constituents in the last," a view which seems hardly to leave room even for judicial control. Three years later as Secretary of the Treasury, Hamilton had brought forward the proposal which soon led to the chartering of the Bank of 1791. The measure precipitated the first great discussion over the interpretation of the new Constitution. Hamilton owned that Congress had no specifically granted power to charter a bank but contended that such an institution was a "necessary and proper" means for carrying out certain of the enumerated powers of the National Government such, for instance, as borrowing money and issuing a currency. For, said he in effect, "necessary and proper" signify "convenient," and the clause was intended to indicate that the National Government should enjoy a wide range of choice in the selection of means for carrying out its enumerated powers. Jefferson, on the other hand, maintained that the "necessary and proper" clause was a restrictive clause, meant to safeguard the rights of the States, that a law in order to be "necessary and proper" must be both "necessary" *and* "proper," and that both terms ought to be construed narrowly. Jefferson's opposition, however, proved unavailing, and the banking institution which was created continued till 1811 without its validity being once tested in the courts.

The second Bank of the United States, whose branch Maryland was now trying to tax, received its charter in 1816 from President Madison. Well might John Quincy Adams exclaim that the "Republicans had outfederalized the Federalists!" Yet the gibe was premature. The country at large was as yet blind to the responsibilities of nationality. That vision of national unity which indubitably underlies the Constitution was after all the vision of an aristocracy conscious of a solidarity of interests transcending state lines. It is equally true that until the Civil War, at the earliest, the great mass of Americans still felt themselves to be first of all citizens of their particular States. Nor did this individualistic bias long remain in want of leadership capable of giving it articulate expression. The amount of political talent which existed within the State of Virginia alone in the first generation of our national history is amazing to contemplate, but this talent unfortunately exhibited one most damaging blemish. The intense individualism of the planter-aristocrat could not tolerate in any possible situation the idea of a control which he could not himself ultimately either direct or reject. In the Virginia and Kentucky resolutions of 1798 and 1799, which regard the Constitution as a compact of sovereign States and the National Government merely as their agent, the particularistic outlook definitely received a constitutional creed which in time was to become, at least in the South, a gloss upon the Constitution regarded as fully as authoritative as the original instrument. This recognition of state sovereignty was, indeed, somewhat delayed by the federalization of the Republican party in consequence of the capture of the National Government by Virginia in 1800. But in 1819 the march toward dissolution and civil war which had begun at the summons of Jefferson was now definitely resumed. This was the year of the congressional struggle over the admission of Missouri, the most important result of which was the discovery by the slave owners that the greatest security of slavery lay in the powers of the States and that its greatest danger lay in those of the National Government. Henceforth the largest property interest of the country stood almost solidly behind State Rights.

It was at this critical moment that chance presented Marshall with the opportunity to place the opposing doctrine of nationalism on the high plane of judicial decision. The arguments in the Bank case,[1] which began on February 22, 1819, and lasted nine days, brought together a "constellation of lawyers" such as had never appeared before in a single case. The Bank was represented by Pinkney, Webster, and Wirt; the State, by Luther Martin, Hopkinson, and Walter Jones of the District of Columbia bar. In arguing for the State, Hopkinson urged the restrictive view of the "necessary and proper" clause and sought to reduce to an absurdity the doctrine of "implied rights." The Bank, continued Hopkinson, "this creature of construction," claims by further implication "the right to enter the territory of a State without its consent" and to establish there a branch; then, by yet another implication, the branch claims exemption from taxation. "It is thus with the famous fig-tree of India, whose branches shoot from the trunk to a considerable distance, then drop to the earth, where they take root and become trees from which also other branches shoot . . . , until gradually a vast surface is covered, and everything perishes

[1] M'Culloch *vs.* Maryland (1819), 4 Wheaton, 316.

in the spreading shade." But even granting that Congress did have the right to charter the Bank, still that fact would not exempt the institution from taxation by any State within which it held property. "The exercise of the one sovereign power cannot be controlled by the exercise of the other."

On the other side, Pinkney made the chief argument in behalf of the Bank. "Mr. Pinkney," says Justice Story, "rose on Monday to conclude the argument; he spoke all that day and yesterday and will probably conclude to-day. I never in my whole life heard a greater speech; it was worth a journey from Salem to hear it; his elocution was excessively vehement; but his eloquence was overwhelming. His language, his style, his figures, his argument, were most brilliant and sparkling. He spoke like a great statesman and patriot and a sound constitutional lawyer. All the cobwebs of sophistryship and metaphysics about State Rights and State Sovereignty he brushed away with a mighty besom."

Pinkney closed on the 3d of March, and on the 6th Marshall handed down his most famous opinion. He condensed Pinkney's three-day argument into a pamphlet which may be easily read by the instructed layman in half an hour, for, as is

9

invariably the case with Marshall, his condensation made for greater clarity. In this opinion he also gives evidence, in their highest form, of his other notable qualities as a judicial stylist: his "tiger instinct for the jugular vein"; his rigorous pursuit of logical consequences; his power of stating a case, wherein he is rivaled only by Mansfield; his scorn of the qualifying "but's," "if's," and "though's"; the pith and balance of his phrasing, a reminiscence of his early days with Pope; the developing momentum of his argument; above all, his audacious use of the *obiter dictum*. Marshall's later opinion in Gibbons *vs*. Ogden is, it is true, in some respects a greater intellectual performance, but it does not equal this earlier opinion in those qualities of form which attract the amateur and stir the admiration of posterity.

At the very outset of his argument in the Bank case Marshall singled out the question the answer to which must control all interpretation of the Constitution: Was the Constitution, as contended by counsel for Maryland, "an act of sovereign and independent States" whose political interests must be jealously safeguarded in its construction, or was it an emanation from the American people and designed for their benefit? Marshall answered that the Constitution, by its own declaration, was "ordained and established" in the name of the people, "in order to form a more perfect union, establish justice, insure domestic tranquillity, and secure the blessings of liberty to themselves and their posterity." Nor did he consider the argument "that the people had already surrendered all their powers to the State Sovereignties and had nothing more to give," a persuasive one, for "surely, the question whether they may resume and modify the power granted to the government does not remain to be settled in this country. Much more might the legitimacy of the General Government be doubted, had it been created by the States. The powers delegated to the State sovereignties were to be exercised by themselves, not by a distinct and independent sovereignty created by them." "The Government of the Union, then," Marshall proceeded, "is emphatically . . . a government of the people. In form and in substance it emanates from them. Its powers are granted by them, and are to be exercised on them, and for their benefit." And what was the nature of this Government? "If any one proposition could command the universal assent of mankind we might expect it would be this: that the government of the Union, though limited in its powers, is supreme within the sphere of its action. This would seem to result necessarily from its nature. It is the government of all; its powers are delegated by all; it represents all and acts for all." However the question had not been left to reason. "The people have in express terms decided it by saying: 'This Constitution and the laws of the United States which shall be made in pursuance thereof . . . shall be the supreme Law of the Land.'"

But a Government which is supreme must have the right to choose the means by which to make its supremacy effective; and indeed, at this point again the Constitution comes to the aid of reason by declaring specifically that Congress may make all laws "necessary and proper" for carrying into execution any of the powers of the General Government. Counsel for Maryland would read this clause as limiting the right which it recognized to the choice only of such means of execution as are indispensable; they would treat the word "necessary" as controlling the clause and to this they would affix the word "absolutely." "Such is the character of human language," rejoins the Chief Justice, "that no word conveys to the mind in all situations, one single definite idea," and the

word "necessary," "like others, is used in various senses," so that its context becomes most material in determining its significance.

And what is its context on this occasion? "The subject is the execution of those great powers on which the welfare of a nation essentially depends." The provision occurs "in a Constitution intended to endure for ages to come and consequently to be adapted to the various crises of human affairs." The purpose of the clause therefore is not to impair the right of Congress "to exercise its best judgment in the selection of measures to carry into execution the constitutional powers of the Government," but rather "to remove all doubts respecting the right to legislate on that vast mass of incidental powers which must be involved in the Constitution, if that instrument be not a splendid bauble. . . . Let the end be legitimate, let it be within the scope of the Constitution and all means which are appropriate, which are plainly adapted to that end, which are not prohibited but consist with the letter and spirit of the Constitution, are constitutional."

But was the Act of Maryland which taxed the Bank in conflict with the Act of Congress which established it? If so, must the State yield to

Congress? In approaching this question Marshall again laid the basis for as sweeping a decision as possible. The terms in which the Maryland statute was couched indicated clearly that it was directed specifically against the Bank, and it might easily have been set aside on that ground. But Marshall went much further and laid down the principle that the instrumentalities of the National Government are never subject to taxation by the States in any form whatsoever, and for two reasons. In the first place, "those means are not given by the people of a particular State . . . but by the people of all the States. They are given by all for the benefit of all," and owe their presence in the State not to the State's permission but to a higher authority. The State of Maryland therefore never had the power to tax the Bank in the first place. Yet waiving this theory, there was, in the second place, flat incompatibility between the Act of Maryland and the Act of Congress, not simply because of the specific operation of the former, but rather because of the implied claim which it made for state authority. "That the power to tax involves the power to destroy," Marshall continued; "that the power to destroy may defeat and render useless the power to create; that there is a plain repugnance in conferring on one government a power to control the constitutional measures of another, which other, with respect to those very measures is declared to be supreme over that which exerts the control, are propositions not to be denied." Nor indeed is the sovereignty of the State confined to taxation. "That is not the only mode in which it might be displayed. The question is in truth, a question of supremacy, and if the right of the States to tax the means employed by the General Government be conceded, the declaration that the Constitution and the laws made in pursuance thereof shall be supreme law of the land, is empty and unmeaning declamation. . . . We are unanimously of opinion," concluded the Chief Justice, "that the law . . . of Maryland, imposing a tax on the Bank of the United States is unconstitutional and void."

Five years later, in the case of Gibbons *vs.* Ogden,[1] known to contemporaries as the "Steamboat case," Marshall received the opportunity to apply his principles of constitutional construction to the power of Congress to regulate "commerce among the States." For a quarter of a century Robert R. Livingston and Robert Fulton and

[1] 9 Wheaton, 1.

their successors had enjoyed from the Legislature of New York a grant of the exclusive right to run steamboats on the waters of the State, and in this case one of their licensees, Ogden, was seeking to prevent Gibbons, who had steamers in the coasting trade under an Act of Congress, from operating them on the Hudson in trade between points in New York and New Jersey. A circumstance which made the case the more critical was that New Jersey and Connecticut had each passed retaliatory statutes excluding from their waters any vessel licensed under the Fulton-Livingston monopoly. The condition of interstate commercial warfare which thus threatened was not unlike that which had originally operated so potently to bring about the Constitution.

The case of Gibbons *vs.* Ogden was argued in the early days of February, 1824, with Attorney-General Wirt and Daniel Webster against the grant, while two famous New York lawyers of the day, Thomas Addis Emmet, brother of the Irish patriot, and Thomas J. Oakley, acted as Ogden's counsel. The arguments have the importance necessarily attaching to a careful examination of a novel legal question of the first magnitude by learned and acute minds, but some of the claims that have been made for these arguments, and especially for Webster's effort, hardly sustain investigation. Webster, never in any case apt to regard his own performance overcritically, seems in later years to have been persuaded that the Chief Justice's opinion "followed closely the track" of his argument on this occasion; and it is true that Marshall expressed sympathy with Webster's contention that Congress may regulate as truly by inaction as by action, since inaction may indicate its wish that the matter go unregulated; but the Chief Justice did not explicitly adopt this idea, and the major part of his opinion was a running refutation of Emmet's argument, which in turn was only an elaboration of Chancellor Kent's opinion upon the same subject in the New York courts.[1] In other words, this was one of those cases in which Marshall's indebtedness to counsel was far less for ideas than for the stimulation which his own powers always received from discussion; and the result is his profoundest, most statesmanlike opinion, from whose doctrines the Court has at times deviated, but only to return to them, until today it is more nearly than ever before the established law on the many points covered by its *dicta*.

[1] See Livingston *vs.* Van Ingen, 9 Johnson, 807 (1812); also Kent's *Commentaries*, I, 432–38.

Marshall pronounced the Fulton-Livingston monopoly inoperative so far as it concerned vessels enrolled under the Act of Congress to engage in the coasting trade; but in arriving at this very simple result his opinion takes the broadest possible range. At the very outset Marshall flatly contradicts Kent's proposition that the powers of the General Government, as representing a grant by sovereignties, must be strictly construed. The Constitution, says he, "contains an enumeration of powers expressly granted by the people to their government," and there is not a word in it which lends any countenance to the idea that these powers should be strictly interpreted. As men whose intentions required no concealment, those who framed and adopted the Constitution "must be understood to have employed words in their natural sense and to have intended what they said"; but if, from the inherent imperfection of language, doubts were at any time to arise "respecting the extent of any given power," then the known purposes of the instrument should control the construction put on its phraseology. "The grant does not convey power which might be beneficial to the grantor if retained by himself . . . but is an investment of power for the general advantage in the hands of agents selected for the purpose, which power can never be exercised by the people themselves, but must be placed in the hands of agents or remain dormant." In no other of his opinions did Marshall so clearly bring out the logical connection between the principle of liberal construction of the Constitution and the doctrine that it is an ordinance of the American people.

Turning then to the Constitution, Marshall asks, "What is commerce?" "Counsel for appellee," he recites, "would limit it to traffic, to buying and selling," to which he answers that "this would restrict a general term . . . to one of its significations. Commerce," he continues, "undoubtedly is traffic, but it is something more — it is intercourse," and so includes navigation. And what is the power of Congress over commerce? "It is the power to regulate, that is, the power to prescribe the rule by which commerce is to be governed." It is a power "complete in itself," exercisable "to its utmost extent," and without limitations "other than are prescribed by the Constitution. . . . If, as has always been understood, the sovereignty of Congress, though limited to specified objects, is plenary as to those objects, the power over commerce with foreign nations and among the several

States is vested in Congress as absolutely as it would be in a single government having in its constitution the same restrictions on the exercise of power as are found in the Constitution of the United States." The power, therefore, is not to be confined by state lines but acts upon its subject-matter wherever it is to be found. "It may, of consequence, pass the jurisdictional line of New York and act upon the very waters to which the prohibition now under consideration applies." It is a power to be exercised within the States and not merely at their frontiers.

But was it sufficient for Marshall merely to define the power of Congress? Must not the power of the State also be considered? At least, Ogden's attorneys had argued, the mere existence in Congress of the power to regulate commerce among the States did not prevent New York from exercising the same power, through legislation operating upon subject matter within its own boundaries. No doubt, he concedes, the States have the right to enact many kinds of laws which will incidentally affect commerce among the States, such for instance as quarantine and health laws, laws regulating bridges and ferries, and so on; but this they do by virtue of their power of "internal police," not by virtue of a "concurrent" power over commerce, foreign and interstate. And, indeed, New York may have granted Fulton and Livingston their monopoly in exercise of this power, in which case its validity would depend upon its not conflicting with an Act of Congress regulating commerce. For should such conflict exist, the State enactment, though passed "in the exercise of its acknowledged sovereignty," must give place in consequence of the supremacy conferred by the Constitution upon all acts of Congress in pursuance of it, over all state laws whatsoever.

The opinion then proceeds to the consideration of the Act of Congress relied upon by Gibbons. This, Ogden's attorneys contended, merely conferred the American character upon vessels already possessed of the right to engage in the coasting trade; Marshall, on the contrary, held that it conferred the right itself, together with the auxiliary right of navigating the waters of the United States; whence it followed that New York was powerless to exclude Gibbons's vessels from the Hudson. Incidentally Marshall indicated his opinion that Congress's power extended to the carriage of passengers as well as of goods and to vessels propelled by steam as well as to those driven by wind. "The one element," said he, "may be as legitimately used as the other for every commercial purpose authorized by the laws of the Union."

Two years later, in the case of Brown *vs*. Maryland,[1] Marshall laid down his famous doctrine that so long as goods introduced into a State in the course of foreign trade remain in the hands of the importer and in the original package, they are not subject to taxation by the State. This doctrine is interesting for two reasons. In the first place, it implies the further principle that an attempt by a State to tax interstate or foreign commerce is tantamount to an attempt to regulate such commerce, and is consequently void. In other words, the principle of the exclusiveness of Congress's power to regulate commerce among the States and with foreign nations, which is advanced by way of *dictum* in Gibbons *vs*. Ogden, becomes in Brown *vs*. Maryland a ground of decision. It is a principle which has proved of the utmost importance in keeping the field of national power clear of encumbering state legislation against the day when Congress should elect to step in and assume effective control. Nor can there be much doubt that the result was intended by the framers of the Constitution.

[1] 12 Wheaton, 419.

In the second place, however, from another point of view this "original package doctrine" is only an extension of the immunity from state taxation established in M'Culloch vs. Maryland for instrumentalities of the National Government. It thus reflects the principle implied by that decision: where power exists to any degree or for any purpose, it exists to every degree and for every purpose; or, to quote Marshall's own words in Brown vs. Maryland, "questions of power do not depend upon the degree to which it may be exercised; if it may be exercised at all, it may be exercised at the will of those in whose hands it is placed." The attitude of the Court nowadays, when it has to deal with state legislation, is very different. It takes the position that abuse of power, in relation to private rights or to commerce, is excess of power and hence demands to be shown the substantial effect of legislation, not its mere formal justification.[1] In short, its inquiry is into facts. On the other hand, when dealing with congressional legislation, the Court has hitherto always followed Marshall's bolder method. Thus Congress may use its taxing

[1] See Justice Bradley's language in 122 U. S., 326; also the more recent case of Western Union Telegraph Company vs. Kan., 216 U. S., 1.

power to drive out unwholesome businesses, perhaps even to regulate labor within the States, and it may close the channels of interstate and foreign commerce to articles deemed by it injurious to the public health or morals.[1] To date this discrepancy between the methods employed by the Court in passing upon the validity of legislation within the two fields of state and national power has afforded the latter a decided advantage.

The great principles which Marshall developed in his interpretation of the Constitution from the side of national power and which after various ups and downs may be reckoned as part of the law of the land today, were the following:

1. The Constitution is an ordinance of the people of the United States, and not a compact of States.

2. Consequently it is to be interpreted with a view to securing a beneficial use of the powers which it creates, not with the purpose of safeguarding the prerogatives of state sovereignty.

3. The Constitution was further designed, as near as may be, "for immortality," and hence was to be "adapted to the various crises of human affairs," to be kept a commodious vehicle of the national life and not made the Procrustean bed of the nation.

4. While the government which the Constitution

[1] See 195 U. S., 27; 188 U. S., 321; 227 U. S., 308. Cf. 247 U. S., 251.

established is one of enumerated powers, as to those powers it is a sovereign government, both in its choice of the means by which to exercise its powers and in its supremacy over all colliding or antagonistic powers.

5. The power of Congress to regulate commerce is an exclusive power, so that the States may not intrude upon this field even though Congress has not acted.

6. The National Government and its instrumentalities are present within the States, not by the tolerance of the States, but by the supreme authority of the people of the United States.[1]

Of these several principles, the first is obviously the most important and to a great extent the source of the others. It is the principle of which Marshall, in face of the rising tide of State Rights, felt himself to be in a peculiar sense the official custodian. It is the principle which he had in mind in his noble plea at the close of the case of Gibbons *vs*. Ogden for a construction of the Constitution capable of maintaining its vitality and usefulness:

Powerful and ingenious minds [run his words], taking as postulates that the powers expressly granted to the Government of the Union are to be contracted by construction into the narrowest possible compass and that the original powers of the States are to be retained if any possible construction will retain them, may by a course

[1] For the application of Marshall's canons of constitutional interpretation in the field of treaty making, see the writer's *National Supremacy* (N. Y., 1913), Chaps. III and IV.

of refined and metaphysical reasoning . . . explain away the Constitution of our country and leave it a magnificent structure indeed to look at, but totally unfit for use. They may so entangle and perplex the understanding as to obscure principles which were before thought quite plain, and induce doubts where, if the mind were to pursue its own course, none would be perceived. In such a case, it is peculiarly necessary to recur to safe and fundamental principles.

CHAPTER VI

THE SANCTITY OF CONTRACTS

MARSHALL'S work was one of conservation in so far as it was concerned with interpreting the Constitution in accord with the intention which its framers had of establishing an efficient National Government. But he found a task of restoration awaiting him in that great field of Constitutional Law which defines state powers in relation to private rights.

To provide adequate safeguards for property and contracts against state legislative power was one of the most important objects of the framers, if indeed it was not the most important. Consider, for instance, a colloquy which occurred early in the Convention between Madison and Sherman of Connecticut. The latter had enumerated "the objects of Union" as follows: "First, defense against foreign danger; secondly, against internal disputes and a resort to force; thirdly, treaties with foreign nations; fourthly, regulating foreign commerce and drawing revenue from it." To this statement Madison demurred. The objects mentioned were important, he admitted, but he "combined with them the necessity of providing more effectually for the securing of private rights and the steady dispensation of justice. Interferences with these were evils which had, more perhaps than anything else, produced this Convention."

Marshall's sympathy with this point of view we have already noted.[1] Nor was Madison's reference solely to the then recent activity of state Legislatures in behalf of the much embarrassed but politically dominant small farmer class. He had also in mind that other and more ancient practice of Legislatures of enacting so-called "special legislation," that is, legislation altering under the standing law the rights of designated parties, and not infrequently to their serious detriment. Usually such legislation took the form of an intervention by the Legislature in private controversies pending in, or already decided by, the ordinary courts, with the result that judgments were set aside, executions canceled, new hearings granted, new rules of evidence introduced, void wills validated, valid contracts

[1] See *supra*, p. 34 ff.

voided, forfeitures pronounced — all by legislative mandate. Since that day the courts have developed an interpretation of the principle of the separation of powers and have enunciated a theory of "due process of law," which renders this sort of legislative abuse quite impossible; but in 1787, though the principle of the separation of powers had received verbal recognition in several of the state Constitutions, no one as yet knew precisely what the term "legislative power" signified, and at that time judicial review did not exist.[1] Hence those who wished to see this nuisance of special legislation abated felt not unnaturally that the relief must come from some source external to the local governments, and they welcomed the movement for a new national Constitution as affording them their opportunity.

The Constitution, in Article I, Section x, forbids the States to "emit bills of credit, make anything but gold and silver a legal tender in payment of debts, pass any bill of attainder, ex post facto law, or law impairing the obligation of contracts." Until 1798, the provision generally regarded as offering the most promising weapon against special

---

[1] On special legislation, see the writer's *Doctrine of Judicial Review* (Princeton, 1914), pp. 36–37, 69–71.

legislation was the *ex post facto* clause. In that year, however, in its decision in Calder *vs.* Bull the Court held that this clause "was not inserted to secure the citizen in his private rights of either property or contracts," but only against certain kinds of penal legislation. The decision roused sharp criticism and the judges themselves seemed fairly to repent of it even in handing it down. Justice Chase, indeed, even went so far as to suggest, as a sort of stop-gap to the breach they were thus creating in the Constitution, the idea that, even in the absence of written constitutional restrictions, the Social Compact as well as "the principles of our free republican governments" afforded judicially enforcible limitations upon legislative power in favor of private rights. Then, in the years immediately following, several state courts, building upon this dictum, had definitely announced their intention of treating as void all legislation which they found unduly to disturb vested rights, especially if it was confined in its operation to specified parties.[1]

Such was still the situation when the case of

[1] In connection with this paragraph, see the writer's article entitled *The Basic Doctrine of American Constitutional Law,* in the *Michigan Law Review,* February, 1914. Marshall once wrote Story regarding

Fletcher *vs.* Peck[1] in 1810 raised before the Supreme Court the question whether the Georgia Legislature had the right to rescind a land grant made by a preceding Legislature. On any of three grounds Marshall might easily have disposed of this case before coming to the principal question. In the first place, it was palpably a moot case; that is to say, it was to the interest of the opposing parties to have the rescinding act set aside. The Court would not today take jurisdiction of such a case, but Marshall does not even suggest such a solution of the question, though Justice Johnson does in his concurring opinion. In the second place, Georgia's own claim to the lands had been most questionable, and consequently her right to grant them to others was equally dubious; but this, too, is an issue which Marshall avoids. Finally, the grant had been procured by corrupt means, but Marshall ruled that this was not a subject the

---

his attitude toward Section x in 1787, as follows: "The questions which were perpetually recurring in the State legislatures and which brought annually into doubt principles which I thought most sacred, which proved that everything was afloat, and that we had no safe anchorage ground, gave a high value in my estimation to that article of the Constitution which imposes restrictions on the States." *Discourse.*

[1] 6 Cranch, 87.

Court might enter upon; and for the ordinary run of cases in which undue influence is alleged to have induced the enactment of a law, the ruling is clearly sound. But this was no ordinary case. The fraud asserted against the grant was a matter of universal notoriety; it was, indeed, the most resounding scandal of the generation; and surely judges may assume to know what is known to all and may act upon their knowledge.

Furthermore, when one turns to the part of Marshall's opinion which deals with the constitutional issue, one finds not a little evidence of personal predilection on the part of the Chief Justice. He starts out by declaring the rescinding act void as a violation of vested rights, of the underlying principles of society and government, and of the doctrine of the separation of powers. Then he apparently realizes that a decision based on such grounds must be far less secure and much less generally available than one based on the words of the Constitution; whereupon he brings forward the obligation of contracts clause. At once, however, he is confronted with the difficulty that the obligation of a contract is the obligation of a contract still to be fulfilled, and that a grant is an executed contract over and done with — *functus officio*. This difficulty he meets by asserting that every grant is attended by an implied contract on the part of the grantor not to reassert his right to the thing granted. This, of course, is a palpable fiction on Marshall's part, though certainly not an unreasonable one. For undoubtedly when a grant is made without stipulation to the contrary, both parties assume that it will be permanent.

The greater difficulty arose from the fact that, whether implied or explicit, the contract before the Court was a *public* one. In the case of private contracts it is easy enough to distinguish the contract, as the agreement between the parties, from the obligation of the contract which comes from the law and holds the parties to their engagements. But what law was there to hold Georgia to her supposed agreement not to rescind the grant she had made? Not the Constitution of the United States unattended by any other law, since it protects the obligation only after it has come into existence. Not the Constitution of Georgia as construed by her own courts, since they had sustained the rescinding act. Only one possibility remained; the State Constitution must be the source of the obligation — yes; but the State Constitution as it was construed by the United States Supreme

Court in this very case, in the light of the "general principles of our political institutions." In short the obligation is a moral one; and this moral obligation is treated by Marshall as having been converted into a legal one by the United States Constitution.

However, Marshall apparently fails to find entire satisfaction in this argument, for he next turns to the prohibition against bills of attainder and *ex post facto* laws with a question which manifests disapproval of the decision in Calder *vs.* Bull. Yet he hesitates to overrule Calder *vs.* Bull, and, indeed, even at the very end of his opinion he still declines to indicate clearly the basis of his decision. The State of Georgia, he says, "was restrained" from the passing of the rescinding act "either by general principles which are common to our free institutions, or by particular provisions of the Constitution of the United States." It was not until nine years after Fletcher *vs.* Peck that this ambiguity was cleared up in the Dartmouth College case in 1819.

The case of the Trustees of Dartmouth College *vs.* Woodward[1] was a New England product and

---

[1] The following account of this case is based on J. M. Shirley's *Dartmouth College Causes* (St. Louis, 1879) and on the official report, 4 Wheaton, 518.

redolent of the soil from which it sprang. In 1754 the Reverend Eleazar Wheelock of Connecticut had established at his own expense a charity school for instructing Indians in the Christian religion; and so great was his success that he felt encouraged to extend the undertaking and to solicit donations in England. Again success rewarded his efforts; and in 1769 Governor Wentworth of New Hampshire, George III's representative granted the new institution, which was now located at Hanover, New Hampshire, a charter incorporating twelve named persons as "The Trustees of Dartmouth College" with the power to govern the institution, appoint its officers, and fill all vacancies in their own body "forever."

For many years after the Revolution, the Trustees of Dartmouth College, several of whom were ministers, reflected the spirit of Congregationalism. Though this form of worship occupied almost the position of a state religion in New Hampshire, early in this period difficulties arose in the midst of the church at Hanover. A certain Samuel Hayes, or Haze, told a woman named Rachel Murch that her character was "as black as Hell," and upon Rachel's complaint to the session, he was "churched" for "breach of the Ninth Commandment and

also for a violation of his covenant agreement."
This incident caused a rift which gradually developed into something very like a schism in the
local congregation, and this internal disagreement
finally produced a split between Eleazar's son, Dr.
John Wheelock, who was now president of Dartmouth College, and the Trustees of the institution.
The result was that in August, 1815, the Trustees
ousted Wheelock.

The quarrel had thus far involved only Calvinists and Federalists, but in 1816 a new element was
brought in by the interference of the Governor
of New Hampshire, William Plumer, formerly a
Federalist but now, since 1812, the leader of the
Jeffersonian party in the State. In a message to
the Legislature dated June 6, 1816, Plumer drew
the attention of that body to Dartmouth College. "All literary establishments," said he, "like
everything human, if not duly attended to, are
subject to decay. . . . As it [the charter of the
College] emanated from royalty, it contained, as
was natural it should, principles congenial to monarchy," and he cited particularly the power of the
Board of Trustees to perpetuate itself. "This last
principle," he continued, "is hostile to the spirit
and genius of a free government. Sound policy

therefore requires that the mode of election should be changed and that Trustees in future should be elected by some other body of men. . . . The College was formed for the *public* good, not for the benefit or emolument of its Trustees; and the right to amend and improve acts of incorporation of this nature has been exercised by all governments, both monarchical and republican."

Plumer sent a copy of his message to Jefferson and received a characteristic answer in reply: "It is replete," said the Republican sage, "with sound principles. . . . The idea that institutions established for the use of the nation cannot be touched nor modified, even to make them answer their end . . . is most absurd. . . . Yet our lawyers and priests generally inculcate this doctrine, and suppose that preceding generations held the earth more freely than we do; had a right to impose laws on us, unalterable by ourselves; . . . in fine, that the earth belongs to the dead and not to the living." And so, too, apparently the majority of the Legislature believed; for by the measure which it promptly passed, in response to Plumer's message, the College was made Dartmouth University, the number of its trustees was increased to twenty-one, the appointment of the additional members being given to the Governor, and a board of overseers, also largely of gubernatorial appointment, was created to supervise all important acts of the trustees.

The friends of the College at once denounced the measure as void under both the State and the United States Constitution and soon made up a test case. In order to obtain the college seal, charter, and records, a mandate was issued early in 1817 by a local court to attach goods, to the value of $50,000, belonging to William H. Woodward, the Secretary and Treasurer of the "University." This was served by attaching a chair "valued at one dollar." The story is also related that authorities of the College, apprehending an argument that the institution had already forfeited its charter on account of having ceased to minister to Indians, sent across into Canada for some of the aborigines, and that three were brought down the river to receive matriculation, but becoming panic-stricken as they neared the town, leaped into the water, swam ashore, and disappeared in the forest. Unfortunately this interesting tale has been seriously questioned.

The attorneys of the College before the Superior Court were Jeremiah Mason, one of the best lawyers of the day, Jeremiah Smith, a former Chief

Justice of New Hampshire, and Daniel Webster. These three able lawyers argued that the amending act exceeded "the rightful ends of legislative power," violated the principle of the separation of powers, and deprived the trustees of their "privileges and immunities" contrary to the "law of the land" clause of the State Constitution, and impaired the obligation of contracts. The last contention stirred Woodward's attorneys, Bartlett and Sullivan, to ridicule. "By the same reasoning," said the latter, "every law must be considered in the nature of a contract, until the Legislature would find themselves in such a labyrinth of contracts, with the United States Constitution over their heads, that not a subject would be left within their jurisdiction"; the argument was an expedient of desperation, he said, a "last straw." The principal contention advanced in behalf of the Act was that the College was "a public corporation," whose "various powers, capacities, and franchises all . . . were to be exercised for the benefit of the public," and were therefore subject to public control. And the Court, in sustaining the Act, rested its decision on the same ground. Chief Justice Richardson conceded the doctrine of Fletcher *vs.* Peck, that the obligation of contracts clause "embraced all contracts relating to private property, whether executed or executory, and whether between individuals, between States, or between States and individuals," but, he urged, "a distinction is to be taken between particular grants by the Legislature of property or privileges to individuals for their own benefit, and grants of power and authority to be exercised for public purposes." Its public character, in short, left the College and its holdings at the disposal of the Legislature.

Of the later proceedings, involving the appeal to Washington and the argument before Marshall, early in March, 1818, tradition has made Webster the central and compelling figure, and to the words which it assigns him in closing his address before the Court has largely been attributed the great legal triumph which presently followed. The story is, at least, so well found that the chronicler of Dartmouth College *vs.* Woodward who should venture to omit it must be a bold man indeed.

The argument ended [runs the tale], Mr. Webster stood for some moments silent before the Court, while every eye was fixed intently upon him. At length, addressing the Chief Justice, he proceeded thus: "This, sir, is my

case. It is the case . . . of every college in our land.
. . . Sir, you may destroy this little institution. . . .
You may put it out. But if you do so, you must carry
through your work! You must extinguish, one after
another, all those greater lights of science, which, for
more than a century have thrown their radiance over
our land. It is, Sir, as I have said, a small college. And
yet there are those who love it — "

Here, the feelings which he had thus far succeeded in
keeping down, broke forth, his lips quivered; his firm
cheeks trembled with emotion, his eyes filled with
tears. . . . The court-room during these two or three
minutes presented an extraordinary spectacle. Chief
Justice Marshall, with his tall and gaunt figure bent
over, as if to catch the slightest whisper, the deep fur-
rows of his cheek expanded with emotion, and his eyes
suffused with tears; Mr. Justice Washington at his side,
with small and emaciated frame, and countenance more
like marble than I ever saw on any other human being.
. . . There was not one among the strong-minded men
of that assembly who could think it unmanly to weep,
when he saw standing before him the man who had
made such an argument, melted into the tenderness of
a child.

Mr. Webster had now recovered his composure, and,
fixing his keen eyes on Chief Justice Marshall, said in
that deep tone with which he sometimes thrilled the
heart of an audience: "Sir, I know not how others may
feel . . . but for myself, when I see my Alma Mater
surrounded, like Cæsar in the Senate house, by those
who are reiterating stab after stab, I would not, for my
right hand, have her turn to me and say, *Et tu quoque
mi fili!* And thou, too, my son!"

11

Whether this extraordinary scene, first described thirty-four years afterward by a putative witness of it, ever really occurred or not, it is today impossible to say.[1] But at least it would be an error to attribute to it great importance. From the same source we have it that at Exeter, too, Webster had made the judges weep — yet they had gone out and decided against him. Judges do not always decide the way they weep!

Of the strictly legal part of his argument Webster himself has left us a synopsis. Fully three-quarters of it dealt with the questions which had been discussed by Mason before the State Supreme Court under the New Hampshire Constitution and was largely irrelevant to the great point at issue at Washington. Joseph Hopkinson, who was now associated with Webster, contributed far more to the content of Marshall's opinion; yet he, too, left one important question entirely to the Chief Justice's ingenuity, as will be indicated shortly. Fortunately for the College its opponents were ill prepared to take advantage of the vulnerable points of its defense. For some unknown reason,

[1] Professor Goodrich of Yale, who is responsible for the story, communicated it to Rufus Choate in 1853. It next appears on Goodrich's authority in Curtis's *Webster*, vol. II, pp. 169–71.

Bartlett and Sullivan, who had carried the day at Exeter, had now given place to William Wirt and John Holmes. Of these the former had just been made Attorney-General of the United States and had no time to give to the case — indeed he admitted that "he had hardly thought of it till it was called on." As for Holmes, he was a "kaleidoscopic politician" and barroom wit, best known to contemporaries as "the noisy eulogist and reputed protégé of Jefferson." A remarkable strategy that, which stood such a person up before John Marshall to plead the right of state Legislatures to dictate the fortunes of liberal institutions!

The arguments were concluded on Thursday, the 12th of March. The next morning the Chief Justice announced that the Court had conferred, that there were different opinions, that some of the judges had not arrived at a conclusion, and that consequently the cause must be continued. Webster, however, who was apt to be much in "the know" of such matters, ventured to place the different judges thus: "The Chief and Washington," he wrote his former colleague Smith, "I have no doubt, are with us. Duvall and Todd perhaps against us; the other three holding up — I cannot much doubt but that Story will be with us in the end, and I think we have much more than an even chance for one of the others."

The friends of the College set promptly to work to bring over the wavering judges. To their dismay they learned that Chancellor James Kent of New York, whose views were known to have great weight with Justices Johnson and Livingston, had expressed himself as convinced by Chief Justice Richardson's opinion that Dartmouth College was a public corporation. Fortunately, however, a little ransacking of the records brought to light an opinion which Kent and Livingston had both signed as early as 1803, when they were members of the New York Council of Revision, and which took the ground that a then pending measure in the New York Legislature for altering the Charter of New York City violated "due process of law." At the same time, Charles Marsh, a friend of both Kent and Webster, brought to the attention of the former Webster's argument before Marshall at Washington in March, 1818. Then came a series of conferences at Albany in which Chancellor Kent, Justice Johnson, President Brown of Dartmouth College, Governor Clinton, and others participated. As a result, the Chancellor owned himself converted to the idea that the College was a private institution.

The new term of court opened on Monday, February 1, 1819. William Pinkney, who in vacation had accepted a retainer from the backers of Woodward, that is, of the State, took his stand on the second day near the Chief Justice, expecting to move for a reargument. Marshall, "turning his blind eye" to the distinguished Marylander, announced that the Court had reached a decision, plucked from his sleeve an eighteen folio manuscript opinion, and began reading it. He held that the College was a "private eleemosynary institution"; that its charter was the outgrowth of a contract between the original donors and the Crown, that the trustees represented the interest of the donors, and that the terms of the Constitution were broad enough to cover and protect this representative interest. The last was the only point on which he confessed a real difficulty. The primary purpose of the constitutional clause, he owned, was to protect "contracts the parties to which have a vested beneficial interest" in them, whereas the trustees had no such interest at stake. But, said he, the case is within the words of the rule, and "must be within its operation likewise, unless there be something in the literal construction" obviously at war with the spirit of the

Constitution, which was far from the fact. For, he continued, "it requires no very critical examination of the human mind to enable us to determine that one great inducement to these gifts is the conviction felt by the giver that the disposition he makes of them is immutable. All such gifts are made in the pleasing, perhaps delusive hope, that the charity will flow forever in the channel which the givers have marked out for it. If every man finds in his own bosom strong evidence of the universality of this sentiment, there can be but little reason to imagine that the framers of our Constitution were strangers to it, and that, feeling the necessity and policy of giving permanence and security to contracts" generally, they yet deemed it desirable to leave this sort of contract subject to legislative interference. Such is Marshall's answer to Jefferson's outburst against "the dead hand."

Characteristically, Marshall nowhere cites Fletcher *vs*. Peck in his opinion, but he builds on the construction there made of the "obligation of contracts" clause as clearly as do his associates, Story and Washington, who cite it again and again in their concurring opinion. Thus he concedes that the British Parliament, in consequence of its unlimited power, might at any time before the Revolution have annulled the charter of the College and so have disappointed the hopes of the donors; but, he adds, *"the perfidy of the transaction would have been universally acknowledged."* Later on, he further admits that at the time of the Revolution the people of New Hampshire succeeded to "the transcendent power of Parliament," as well as to that of the King, with the result that a repeal of the charter before 1789 could have been contested only under the State Constitution. "But the Constitution of the United States," he continues, "has imposed this additional limitation, that the Legislature of a State shall pass no act 'impairing the obligation of contracts.'" In short, as in Fletcher *vs.* Peck, what was originally a moral obligation is regarded as having been lifted by the Constitution into the full status of a legal one, and this time without any assistance from "the general principles of our free institutions."

How is the decision of the Supreme Court in the case of Dartmouth College *vs.* Woodward to be assessed today? Logically the basis of it was repudiated by the Court itself within a decade, albeit the rule it lays down remained unaffected. Historically it is equally without basis, for the intention of the obligation of contracts clause, as the evidence amply shows, was to protect private executory contracts, and especially contracts of debt.[1] In actual practice, on the other hand, the decision produced one considerable benefit: in the words of a contemporary critic, it put private institutions of learning and charity out of the reach of "legislative despotism and party violence."

But doubtless, the critic will urge, by the same sign this decision also put profit-seeking corporations beyond wholesome legislative control. But is this a fact? To begin with, such a criticism is clearly misdirected. As we have just seen, the New Hampshire Superior Court itself would have felt that Fletcher *vs.* Peck left it no option but to declare the amending act void, had Dartmouth College been, say, a gas company; and this was in all probability the universal view of bench and bar in 1819. Whatever blame there is should therefore be awarded the earlier decision. But, in the second place, there does not appear after all to be so great measure of blame to be awarded. The opinion in Dartmouth College *vs.* Woodward leaves it perfectly clear that legislatures may reserve the right to alter or repeal at will the charters they grant.

[1] Much of the evidence is readily traceable through the Index to Max Farrand's *Records of the Federal Convention.*

If therefore alterations and repeals have not been as frequent as public policy has demanded, whose fault is it?

Perhaps, however, it will be argued that the real mischief of the decision has consisted in its effect upon the state Legislatures themselves, the idea being that large business interests, when offered the opportunity of obtaining irrepealable charters, have frequently found it worth their while to assail frail legislative virtue with irresistible temptation. The answer to this charge is a "confession in avoidance"; the facts alleged are true enough but hardly to the point. Yet even if they were, what is to be said of that other not uncommon incident of legislative history, the legislative "strike," whereby corporations not protected by irrepealable charters are blandly confronted with the alternative of having their franchises mutilated or of paying handsomely for their immunity? So the issue seems to resolve itself into a question of taste regarding two species of legislative "honesty." Does one prefer that species which, in the words of the late Speaker Reed, manifests itself in "staying bought," or that species which flowers in legislative blackmail? The truth of the matter is that Marshall's decision has been condemned by ill-informed or

were convinced that every *man* in America was secured in all his rights, we should be ready to sacrifice this substantial good to the phantom of *state* sovereignty."

Lastly, these decisions brought a certain theoretical support to the Union. Marshall himself did not regard the Constitution as a compact between the States; if a compact at all, it was a compact among individuals, a social compact. But a great and increasing number of his countrymen took the other view. How unsafe, then, it would have been from the standpoint of one concerned for the integrity of the Union, to distinguish public contracts from private on the ground that the former, in the view of the Constitution, had less obligation!

CHAPTER VII

THE MENACE OF STATE RIGHTS

MARSHALL's reading of the Constitution may be summarized in a phrase: it transfixed State Sovereignty with a two-edged sword, one edge of which was inscribed "National Supremacy," and the other "Private Rights." Yet State Sovereignty, ever reanimated by the democratic impulse of the times, remained a serpent which was scotched but not killed. To be sure, this dangerous enemy to national unity had failed to secure for the state Legislatures the right to interpret the Constitution with authoritative finality; but its argumentative resources were still far from exhausted, and its political resources were steadily increasing. It was still capable of making a notable resistance even in withdrawing itself, until it paused in its recoil and flung itself forward in a new attack.

The connecting link between the Supreme Court and the state courts has already been pointed out to be Section xxv of the Act of 1789 organizing the Federal Judiciary.[1] This section provides, in effect, that when a suit is brought in a state court under a state law, and the party against whom it is brought claims some right under a national law or treaty or under the Constitution itself, the highest state court into which the case can come must either sustain such a claim or consent to have its decision reviewed, and possibly reversed, by the Supreme Court. The defenders of State Rights at first applauded this arrangement because it left to the local courts the privilege of sharing a jurisdiction which could have been claimed exclusively by the Federal Courts. But when State Rights began to grow into State Sovereignty, a different attitude developed, and in 1814 the Virginia Court of Appeals, in the case of Hunter *vs.* Martin,[2] pronounced Section xxv void, though, in order not to encourage the disloyal tendencies then rampant in New England, the decision was not published until after the Treaty of Ghent, in February, 1815.

The head and front of the Virginia court at this time was Spencer Roane, described as "the most

[1] See pages 14–15.

[2] 4 Munford (Va.), 1. See also William E. Dodd's article on *Chief Justice Marshall and Virginia* in *American Historical Review*, vol. XII, p. 776.

powerful politician in the State," an ardent Jeffersonian, and an enemy of Marshall on his own account, for had Ellsworth not resigned so inopportunely, late in 1800, and had Jefferson had the appointment of his successor, Roane would have been the man. His opinion in Hunter *vs.* Martin disclosed personal animus in every line and was written with a vehemence which was more likely to discomfit a grammarian than its designed victims; but it was withal a highly ingenious plea. At one point Roane enjoyed an advantage which would not be his today when so much more gets into print, for the testimony of Madison's *Journal*, which was not published till 1840, is flatly against him on the main issue. In 1814, however, the most nearly contemporaneous evidence as to the intention of the framers of the Constitution was that of the *Federalist*, which Roane stigmatizes as "a mere newspaper publication written in the heat and fury of the battle," largely by "a supposed favorer of a consolidated government." This description not only overlooks the obvious effort of the authors of the *Federalist* to allay the apprehensions of state jealousy but it also conveniently ignores Madison's part in its composition. Indeed, the *enfant terrible* of State Rights, the Madison of 1787–88, Roane would fain conceal behind the Madison of ten years later; and the Virginia Resolutions of 1798 and the Report of 1799 he regards the earliest "just exposition of the principles of the Constitution."

To the question whether the Constitution gave "any power to the Supreme Court of the United States to reverse the judgment of the supreme court of a State," Roane returned an emphatic negative. His argument may be summarized thus: The language of Article III of the Constitution does not regard the state courts as composing a part of the judicial organization of the General Government; and the States, being sovereign, cannot be stripped of their power merely by implication. Conversely, the General Government is a government over individuals and is therefore expected to exercise its powers solely through its own organs. To be sure, the judicial power of the United States extends to "all cases arising" under the Constitution and the laws of the United States. But in order to come within this description, a case must not merely involve the construction of the Constitution or laws of the United States; it must have been instituted in the United States courts, and not in those of another Government. Further, the Constitution and the acts of Congress "in pursuance thereof" are "the supreme law of the land," and "the judges in every State" are "bound thereby, anything in the Constitution or laws of any State to the contrary notwithstanding." But they are bound as state judges and only as such; and what the Constitution is, or what acts of Congress are "in pursuance" of it, is for them to declare without any correction or interference by the courts of another jurisdiction. Indeed, it is through the power of its courts to say finally what acts of Congress are constitutional and what are not, that the State is able to exercise its right of arresting within its boundaries unconstitutional measures of the General Government. For the legislative nullification of such measures proposed by the Virginia and Kentucky resolutions is thus substituted judicial nullification by the local judiciaries.

In Martin *vs.* Hunter's Lessee,[1] which was decided in February, 1816, Story, speaking for the Court, undertook to answer Roane. Roane's major premise he met with flat denial: "It is a mistake," he asserts, "that the Constitution was not designed to operate upon States in their corporate capacities. It is crowded with provisions

---

[1] 1 Wheaton, 304. Marshall had an indirect interest in the case. See *supra*, pp. 44–45.

which restrain or annul the sovereignty of the States in some of the highest branches of their prerogatives." The greater part of the opinion, however, consisted of a minute examination of the language of Article III of the Constitution. In brief, he pointed out that while Congress "may . . . establish" inferior courts and, therefore, may not, it was made imperative that the judicial power of the United States "shall extend to all cases arising . . . under" the Constitution and acts of Congress. If, therefore, Congress should exercise its option and not establish inferior courts, in what manner, he asked, could the purpose of the Constitution be realized except by providing appeals from the state courts to the United States Supreme Court? But more than that, the practical consequences of the position taken by the Virginia Court of Appeals effectually refuted it. That there should be as many versions of the Constitution, laws, and treaties as there are States in the Union was certainly never intended by the framers, nor yet that plaintiffs alone should say when resort should be had to the national tribunals, which were designed for the benefit of all.

If Story's argument is defective at any point, it is in its failure to lay down a clear definition of "cases arising under this Constitution," and this defect in constitutional interpretation is supplied five years later in Marshall's opinion in Cohens *vs.* Virginia.[1] The facts of this famous case were as follows: Congress had established a lottery for the District of Columbia, for which the Cohens had sold tickets in Virginia. They had thus run foul of a state law prohibiting such transactions and had been convicted of the offense in the Court of Quarterly Sessions of Norfolk County and fined one hundred dollars. From this judgment they were now appealing under Section xxv.

Counsel for the State of Virginia again advanced the principles which had been developed by Roane in Hunter *vs.* Martin but urged in addition that this particular appeal rendered Virginia a defendant contrary to Article XI of the Amendments. Marshall's summary of their argument at the outset of his opinion is characteristic: "They maintain," he said, "that the nation does not possess a department capable of restraining peaceably, and by authority of law, any attempts which may be made by a part against the legitimate powers of the whole, and that the government is reduced to the alternative of submitting to such attempts or of

[1] 6 Wheaton, 264.

resisting them by force. They maintain that the Constitution of the United States has provided no tribunal for the final construction of itself or of the laws or treaties of the nation, but that this power must be exercised in the last resort by the courts of every State in the Union. That the Constitution, laws, and treaties may receive as many constructions as there are States; and that this is not a mischief, or, if a mischief, is irremediable."

The cause of such absurdities, Marshall continued, was a conception of State Sovereignty contradicted by the very words of the Constitution, which assert its supremacy, and that of all acts of Congress in pursuance of it, over all conflicting state laws whatsoever. "This," he proceeded to say, "is the authoritative language of the American People, and if gentlemen please, of the American States. It marks, with lines too strong to be mistaken, the characteristic distinction between the Government of the Union and those of the States. The General Government, though limited as to its objects, is supreme with respect to those objects. This principle is a part of the Constitution, and if there be any who deny its necessity, none can deny its authority." Nor was this to say that the Constitution is unalterable. "The people make the Constitution, and the people can unmake it. It is the creature of their own will, and lives only by their will. But this supreme and irresistible power to make or unmake resides only in the whole body of the people, not in any subdivision of them. The attempt of any of the parts to exercise it is usurpation, and ought to be repelled by those to whom the people have delegated their power of repelling it."

Once Marshall had swept aside the irrelevant notion of State Sovereignty, he proceeded with the remainder of his argument without difficulty. Counsel for Virginia had contended that "a case arising under the Constitution or a law must be one in which a party comes into court to demand something conferred on him by the Constitution or a law"; but this construction Marshall held to be "too narrow." "A case in law or equity consists of the right of the one party as well as of the other, and may truly be said to arise under the Constitution or a law of the United States *whenever its correct decision depends on the construction of either.*" From this it followed that Section xxv was a measure necessary and proper for extending the judicial power of the United States appellately to such cases whenever they were first brought in a state court. Nor did Article XI of the Amendments nullify the power thus conferred upon the Court in a case which the State itself had instituted, for in such a case the appeal taken to the national tribunal was only another stage in an action "begun and prosecuted," not against the State, but by the State. The contention of Virginia was based upon the assumption that the Federal and the State Judiciaries constituted independent systems for the enforcement of the Constitution, the national laws, and treaties, and such an assumption Marshall held to be erroneous. For the purposes of the Constitution the United States "form a single nation," and in effecting these purposes the Government of the Union may "legitimately control all individuals or governments within the American territory."

"Our opinion in the Bank Case," Marshall had written Story from Richmond in 1819, a few weeks after M'Culloch vs. Maryland, "has roused the sleeping spirit of Virginia, if indeed it ever sleeps." Cohens vs. Virginia, in 1821, produced an even more decided reaction. Jefferson, now in retirement, had long since nursed his antipathy for the Federal Judiciary to the point of monomania. It was in his eyes "a subtle corps of sappers and

miners constantly working underground to under-
mine our confederated fabric"; and this latest assault upon the rights of the States seemed to him,
though perpetrated in the usual way, the most
outrageous of all: "An opinion is huddled up in
conclave, perhaps by a majority of one, delivered
as if unanimous, and with the silent acquiescence
of lazy or timid associates, by a crafty chief judge,
who sophisticates the law to his own mind by the
turn of his own reasoning."

Roane, Jefferson's protégé, was still more violent and wrote a series of unrestrained papers at
this time in the Richmond *Enquirer*, under the
pseudonym "Algernon Sidney." Alluding to these,
Marshall wrote Story that "their coarseness and
malignity would designate the author of them if
he was not avowed." Marshall himself thought to
answer Roane, but quickly learned that the Virginia press was closed to that side of the question. He got his revenge, however, by obtaining
the exclusion of Roane's effusions from Hall's *Law
Journal*, an influential legal periodical published in
Philadelphia. But the personal aspect of the controversy was the least important. "A deep design,"
Marshall again wrote his colleague, "to convert
our Government into a mere league of States has

taken hold of a powerful and violent party in Virginia. The attack upon the judiciary is in fact an attack upon the Union." Nor was Virginia the only State where this movement was formidable, and an early effort to repeal Section xxv was to be anticipated.

That the antijudicial movement was extending to other States was indeed apparent. The decision in Sturges vs. Crowinshield[1] left for several years the impression that the States could not pass bankruptcy laws even for future contracts and consequently afforded a widespread grievance. Ohio had defied the ruling in M'Culloch vs. Maryland, and her Treasurer was languishing in jail by the mandate of the Federal Circuit Court. Kentucky had a still sharper grievance in the decision in Green vs. Biddle,[2] which invalidated a policy she had been pursuing for nearly a quarter of a century with reference to squatters' holdings; and what made the decision seem the more outrageous was the mistaken belief that it had represented the views of only a minority of the justices.

The Legislatures of the aggrieved States were soon in full hue and cry at the heels of the Court; and from them the agitation quickly spread to

[1] 4 Wheaton, 122.   [2] 8 Wheaton, 1.

Congress.[1] On December 12, 1821, Senator Johnson of Kentucky proposed an amendment to the Constitution which was intended to substitute the Senate for the Supreme Court in all constitutional cases. In his elaborate speech in support of his proposition, Johnson criticized at length the various decisions of the Court but especially those grounded on its interpretation of the "obligation of contracts" clause. More than that, however, he denied *in toto* the rights of the Federal Courts to pass upon the constitutionality either of acts of Congress or of state legislative measures. So long as judges were confined to the field of jurisprudence, the principles of which were established and immutable, judicial independence was all very well, said Johnson, but "the science of politics was still in its infancy"; and in a republican system of government its development should be entrusted to those organs which were responsible to the people. Judges were of no better clay than other folk. "Why, then, " he asked, "should they be considered any more infallible, or their decisions any less subject to investigation and revision?"

[1] For a good review of the contemporary agitation aroused by Marshall's decisions, see two articles by Charles Warren in the *American Law Review*, vol. XLVII, pp. 1 and 161.

Furthermore, "courts, like cities, and villages, or like legislative bodies, wil ometimes have their leaders; and it may happ that a single individual will be the prime cause of a decision to overturn the deliberate act of a whole State or of the United States; yet we are admonished to receive their opinions as the ancients did the responses of the Delphic oracle, or the Jews, with more propriety, the communications from Heaven delivered by *Urim* and *Thummim* to the High Priest of God's chosen people."

For several years after this, hardly a session of Congress convened in which there was not introduced some measure for the purpose either of curbing the Supreme Court or of curtailing Marshall's influence on its decisions. One measure, for example, proposed the repeal of Section xxv; another, the enlargement of the Court from seven to ten judges; another, the requirement that any decision setting aside a state law must have the concurrence of five out of seven judges; another, the allowance of appeals to the Court on decisions adverse to the constitutionality of state laws as well as on decisions sustaining them. Finally, in January, 1826, a bill enlarging the Court to ten judges passed the House by a vote of 132 to 27.

In the Senate, Rowan of Kentucky moved an amendment requiring in all cases the concurrence of seven of the proposed ten judges. In a speech which was typical of current criticism of the Court he bitterly assailed the judges for the protection they had given the Bank — that "political juggernaut," that "creature of the perverted corporate powers of the Federal Government" — and he described the Court itself as "placed above the control of the will of the people, in a state of disconnection with them, inaccessible to the charities and sympathies of human life." The amendment failed, however, and in the end the bill itself was rejected.

Yet a proposition to swamp the Court which received the approval of four-fifths of the House of Representatives cannot be lightly dismissed as an aberration. Was it due to a fortuitous coalescence of local grievances, or was there a general underlying cause? That Marshall's principles of constitutional law did not entirely accord with the political and economic life of the nation at this period must be admitted. The Chief Justice was at once behind his times and ahead of them. On the one hand, he was behind his times because he failed to appreciate adequately the fact that freedom was necessary to frontier communities in meeting their peculiar problems — a freedom which the doctrine of State Rights promised them — and so he had roused Kentucky's wrath by the pedantic and, as the Court itself was presently forced to admit, unworkable decision in Green *vs.* Biddle. Then on the other hand, the nationalism of this period was of that negative kind which was better content to worship the Constitution than to make a really serviceable application of the national powers. After the War of 1812 the great and growing task which confronted the rapidly expanding nation was that of providing adequate transportation, and had the old federalism from which Marshall derived his doctrines been at the helm, this task would undoubtedly have been taken over by the National Government. By Madison's veto of the Cumberland Road Bill, however, in 1816, this enterprise was handed over to the States; and they eagerly seized upon it after the opening of the Erie Canal in 1825 and the perception of the immense success of the venture. Later, to be sure, the panic of 1837 transferred the work of railroad and canal building to the hands of private capital but, after all, without altering greatly the constitutional problem. For with corporations to be chartered, endowed with the power of eminent domain, and adequately regulated, local policy obviously called for widest latitude.

Reformers are likely to count it a grievance that the courts do not trip over themselves in an endeavor to keep abreast with what is called "progress." But the true function of courts is not to reform, but to maintain a definite *status quo*. The Constitution defined a *status quo* the fundamental principles of which Marshall considered sacred. At the same time, even his obstinate loyalty to "the intentions of the framers" was not impervious to facts nor unwilling to come to terms with them, and a growing number of his associates were ready to go considerably farther.

While the agitation in Congress against the Court was at its height, Marshall handed down his decision in Gibbons *vs*. Ogden, and shortly after, that in Osborn *vs*. United States Bank.[1] In the latter case, which was initiated by the Bank, the plaintiff in error, who was Treasurer of the State of Ohio, brought forward Article XI of the Amendments to the Constitution as a bar to the action, but Marshall held that this Amendment did not prevent a state officer from being sued for acts

[1] 9 Wheaton, 738.

done in excess of his rightful powers. He also reiterated and amplified the principles of M'Culloch vs. Maryland. Three years later he gave his opinions in Brown vs. Maryland and Ogden vs. Saunders.[1] In the former Marshall's opinion was dissented from by a single associate, but in the latter the Chief Justice found himself for the first and only time in his entire incumbency in the rôle of dissenter in a constitutional case. The decision of the majority, speaking through Justice Washington, laid down the principle that the obligation of a private executory contract cannot be said to be "impaired" in a constitutional sense by the adverse effect of legislative acts antedating the making of the contract; and thus the dangerous ambiguity of Sturges vs. Crowinshield was finally resolved in favor of the States.

In the course of the next few years the Court, speaking usually through the Chief Justice, decided several cases on principles favoring local interest, sometimes indeed curtailing the operation of previously established principles. For example, the Court held that, in the absence of specific legislation by Congress to the contrary, a State may erect a dam across navigable waters of the

[1] 12 Wheaton, 213.

United States for local purposes[1]; that the mere grant of a charter to a corporation does not prevent the State from taxing such corporation on its franchises, notwithstanding that "the power to tax involves the power to destroy"[2]; that the Federal Courts have no right to set a state enactment aside on the ground that it had divested vested rights, unless it had done so through impairing the obligation of contracts[3]; that the first eight Amendments to the Constitution do not limit state power, but only Federal power[4]; that decisions adverse to state laws must have the concurrence of a majority of the Court.[5]

Despite all these concessions which he made to the rising spirit of the times, Marshall found his last years to be among the most trying of his chief justiceship. Jackson, who was now President, felt himself the chosen organ of "the People's will" and was not disposed to regard as binding anybody's interpretation of the Constitution except his own. The West and Southwest, the pocket boroughs of

[1] Wilson *vs.* Blackbird Creek Marsh Company (1829), 2 Peters, 245.
[2] Providence Bank *vs.* Billings (1830), 4 Peters, 514.
[3] Satterlee *vs.* Matthewson (1829), 2 Peters, 380; and Watson *vs.* Mercer (1834), 8 Peters, 110.
[4] Barron *vs.* Baltimore (1833), 7 Peters, 243.
[5] See in this connection the Chief Justice's remarks in Briscoe *vs.* Bank of Kentucky, 8 Peters, 118.

the new Administration, were now deep in land speculation and clamorous for financial expedients which the Constitution banned. John Taylor of Caroline had just finished his task of defining the principles of constitutional construction which were requisite to convert the Union into a league of States and had laid his work at the feet of Calhoun. Taylor was a candid man and frankly owned the historical difficulties in the way of carrying out his purpose; but Calhoun's less scrupulous dialectic swept aside every obstacle that stood in the way of attributing to the States the completest sovereignty.

In Craig *vs.* Missouri (1830) [1] the Court was confronted with a case in which a State had sought to evade the prohibition of the Constitution against the emission of bills of credit by establishing loan offices with authority to issue loan certificates intended to circulate generally in dimensions of fifty cents to ten dollars and to be receivable for taxes. A plainer violation of the Constitution would be difficult to imagine. Yet Marshall's decision setting aside the act was followed by a renewed effort to procure the repeal of Section xxv of the Judiciary Act. The discussion of the proposal

[1] 4 Peters, 410.

threw into interesting contrast two points of view. The opponents of this section insisted upon regarding constitutional cases as controversies between the United States and the States in their corporate capacities; its advocates, on the other hand, treated the section as an indispensable safeguard of private rights. In the end, the latter point of view prevailed: the bill to repeal, which had come up in the House, was rejected by a vote of 138 to 51, and of the latter number all but six came from Southern States, and more than half of them from natives of Virginia.

Meantime the Supreme Court had become involved in controversy with Georgia on account of a series of acts which that State had passed extending its jurisdiction over the Cherokee Indians in violation of the national treaties with this tribe. In Corn Tassel's case, the appellant from the Georgia court to the United States Supreme Court was hanged in defiance of a writ of error from the Court. In Cherokee Nation *vs.* Georgia, the Court itself held that it had no jurisdiction. Finally, in 1832, in Worcester *vs.* Georgia,[1] the Court was confronted squarely with the question of the validity of the Georgia acts. The State put in no appearance,

[1] 6 Peters, 515.

13

the acts were pronounced void, and the decision went unenforced. When Jackson was asked what effort the Executive Department would make to back up the Court's mandate, he is reported to have said: "John Marshall has made his decision; now let him enforce it."

Marshall began to see the Constitution and the Union crumbling before him. "I yield slowly and reluctantly to the conviction," he wrote Story, late in 1832, "that our Constitution cannot last. . . . Our opinions [in the South] are incompatible with a united government even among ourselves. The Union has been prolonged this far by miracles." A personal consideration sharpened his apprehension. He saw old age at hand and was determined "not to hazard the disgrace of continuing in office a mere inefficient pageant," but at the same time he desired some guarantee of the character of the person who was to succeed him. At first he thought of remaining until after the election of 1832; but Jackson's reëlection made him relinquish altogether the idea of resignation.

A few months later, in consequence of the Administration's vigorous measures against nullification in South Carolina, things were temporarily wearing a brighter aspect. Yet that the fundamental elements of the situation had been thereby altered, Marshall did not believe. "To men who think as you and I do," he wrote Story, toward the end of 1834, "the present is gloomy enough; and the future presents no cheering prospect. In the South . . . those who support the Executive do not support the Government. They sustain the personal power of the President, but labor incessantly to impair the legitimate powers of the Government. Those who oppose the rash and violent measures of the Executive . . . are generally the bitter enemies of Constitutional Government. Many of them are the avowed advocates of a league; and those who do not go the whole length, go a great part of the way. What can we hope for in such circumstances?"

Yet there was one respect in which the significance of Marshall's achievement must have been as clear to himself as it was to his contemporaries. He had failed for the time being to establish his definition of national power, it is true, but he had made the Supreme Court one of the great political forces of the country. The very ferocity with which the pretensions of the Court were assailed in certain quarters was indirect proof of its power, but there was also direct testimony of a high order.

In 1830 Alexis de Tocqueville, the French statesman, visited the United States just as the rough
frontier democracy was coming into its own. Only
through the Supreme Court, in his opinion, were
the forces of renewal and growth thus liberated to
be kept within the bounds set by existing institutions. "The peace, the prosperity, and the very
existence of the Union," he wrote, "are vested in
the hands of the seven Federal judges. Without
them the Constitution would be a dead letter: the
Executive appeals to them for assistance against
the encroachments of the legislative power; the
Legislature demands their protection against the
assaults of the Executive; they defend the Union
from the disobedience of the States, the States from
the exaggerated claims of the Union, the public
interest against private interests and the conservative spirit of stability against the fickleness of
the democracy." The contrast between these ob-
servations and the disheartened words in which Jay
declined renomination to the chief justiceship in
1801 gives perhaps a fair measure of Marshall's
accomplishment.

Of the implications of the accomplishment of the
great Chief Justice for the political life of the country, let De Tocqueville speak again: "Scarcely any

political question arises in the United States which is not resolved sooner, or later, into a judicial question. Hence all parties are obliged to borrow in their daily controversies the ideas, and even the language peculiar to judicial proceedings. . . . The language of the law thus becomes, in some measure, a vulgar tongue; the spirit of law, which is produced in the schools and courts of justice, gradually penetrates beyond their walls into the bosom of society, where it descends to the lowest classes, so that at last the whole people contract the habits and the tastes of the judicial magistrate."

In one respect, however, De Tocqueville erred. American "legalism," that curious infusion of politics with jurisprudence, that mutual consultation of public opinion and established principles, which in the past has so characterized the course of discussion and legislation in America, is traceable to origins long antedating Marshall's chief justiceship. On the other hand, there is no public career in American history which ever built so largely upon this pervasive trait of the national outlook as did Marshall's, or which has contributed so much to render it effective in palpable institutions.

CHAPTER VIII

AMONG FRIENDS AND NEIGHBORS

IT is a circumstance of no little importance that the founder of American Constitutional Law was in tastes and habit of life a simple countryman. To the establishment of National Supremacy and the Sanctity of Contracts Marshall brought the support not only of his office and his command of the art of judicial reasoning but also the whole-souled democracy and unpretentiousness of the fields. And it must be borne in mind that Marshall was on view before his contemporaries as a private citizen rather more of the time, perhaps, than as Chief Justice. His official career was, in truth, a somewhat leisurely one. Until 1827 the term at Washington rarely lasted over six weeks and subsequently not over ten weeks. In the course of his thirty-four years on the Bench, the Court handed down opinions in over 1100 cases, which is probably about four times the number of opinions now handed down at a single term; and of this number Marshall spoke for the Court in about half the cases. Toward the middle of March, he left Washington for Richmond, and on the 22d of May opened court in his own circuit. Then, three weeks later, if the docket permitted, he went on to Raleigh to hold court there for a few days. The summers he usually spent on the estate which he inherited from his father at Fauquier, or else he went higher up into the mountains to escape malaria. But by the 22d of November at the latest he was back once more in Richmond for court, and at the end of December for a second brief term he again drove to Raleigh in his high-wheeled gig. With his return to Washington early in February he completed the round of his judicial year.

The entire lack of pageantry and circumstance which attended these journeyings of his is nowhere more gaily revealed than in the following letter to his wife, which is now published for the first time through the kindness of Mr. Beveridge:

RAWLEIGH, Jan.ʸ 2ᵈ, 1803.

MY DEAREST POLLY

You will laugh at my vexation when you hear the various calamities that have befallen me. In the first place when I came to review my funds, I had the mortification to discover that I had lost 15 silver dollars out of my waist coat pocket. They had worn through the various mendings the pocket had sustained and sought their liberty in the sands of Carolina.

I determined not to vex myself with what could not be remedied & ordered Peter to take out my cloaths that I might dress for court when to my astonishment & grief after fumbling several minutes in the portmanteau, starting [sic] at vacancy, & sweating most profusely he turned to me with the doleful tidings that I had no pair of breeches. You may be sure this piece of intelligence was not very graciously received; however, after a little scolding, I determined to make the best of my situation & immediately set out to get a pair made.

I thought I should be a sans-culotte only one day & that for the residue of the term I might be well enough dressed for the appearance on the first day to be forgotten.

But, the greatest of evils, I found, was followed by still greater. Not a taylor in town could be prevailed on to work for me. They were all so busy that it was impossible to attend to my wants however pressing they might be, & I have the extreme mortification to pass the whole time without that important article of dress I have mentioned. I have no alleviation for this misfortune but the hope that I shall be enabled in four or five days to commence my journey homeward & that I shall have the pleasure of seeing you & our dear children in eight or nine days after this reaches you.

In the meantime, I flatter myself that you are well and happy.

Adieu my dearest Polly
I am your own affectionate,
J. MARSHALL.

Marshall erected his Richmond home, called "Shockoe Hill," in 1793 on a plot of ground which he had purchased four years earlier. Here, as his eulogist has said, was "the scene of his real triumphs." At an early date his wife became a nervous invalid, and his devotion to her brought out all the finest qualities of his sound and tender nature. "It is," says Mr. Beveridge, "the most marked characteristic of his entire private life and is the one thing which differentiates him sharply from the most eminent men of that heroic but socially free-and-easy period." From his association with his wife Marshall derived, moreover, an opinion of the sex "as the friends, the companions, and the equals of man" which may be said to have furnished one of his few points of sympathetic contact with American political radicalism in his later years. The satirist of woman, says Story, "found no sympathy in his bosom," and "he was still farther above the commonplace flatteries by which frivolity seeks to administer aliment to personal vanity, or vice to make its approaches for baser purposes. He spoke to the sex when present, as he spoke of them when absent, in language of just appeal to their understandings, their tastes, and their duties."

Marshall's relations with his neighbors were the happiest possible. Every week, when his judicial duties permitted or the more "laborious relaxation" of directing his farm did not call him away, he attended the meetings of the Barbecue Club in a fine grove just outside the city, to indulge in his favorite diversion of quoits. The Club consisted of thirty of the most prominent men of Richmond, judges, lawyers, doctors, clergymen, and merchants. To quoits was added the inducement of an excellent repast of which roast pig was the *pièce de résistance*. Then followed a dessert of fruit and melons, while throughout a generous stock of porter, toddy, and of punch "from which water was carefully excluded," was always available to relieve thirst. An entertaining account of a meeting of the Club at which Marshall and his friend Wickham were the caterers has been thus preserved for us:

At the table Marshall announced that at the last meeting two members had introduced politics, a forbidden subject, and had been fined a basket of champagne, and that this was now produced, as a warning to evil-doers; as the club seldom drank this article, they had no champagne glasses, and must drink it in tumblers. Those who played quoits retired after a while for a game. Most of the members had smooth, highly polished brass quoits. But Marshall's were large, rough, heavy, and of iron, such as few of the members could throw well from hub to hub. Marshall himself threw them with great success and accuracy, and often "rang the meg." On this occasion Marshall and the Rev. Mr. Blair led the two parties of players. Marshall played first, and rang the meg. Parson Blair did the same, and his quoit came down plumply on top of Marshall's. There was uproarious applause, which drew out all the others from the dinner; and then came an animated controversy as to what should be the effect of this exploit. They all returned to the table, had another bottle of champagne, and listened to arguments, one from Marshall, pro se, and one from Wickham for Parson Blair. [Marshall's] argument is a humorous companion piece to any one of his elaborate judicial opinions. He began by formulating the question, "Who is winner when the adversary quoits are on the meg at the same time?" He then stated the facts, and remarked that the question was one of the true construction and applications of the rules of the game. The first one ringing the meg has the advantage. No other can succeed who does not begin by displacing this first one. The parson, he willingly allowed, deserves to rise higher and higher in everybody's esteem; but then he mustn't do it by getting on another's back in this fashion. That is more like leapfrog than quoits. Then, again, the legal maxim, *Cujus est solum, ejus est usque ad cœlum* — his own right as first occupant extends to the vault of heaven; no opponent can gain any advantage by squatting on his back. He must either bring a writ of ejectment, or drive him out *vi et armis*. And then, after further argument of the same sort, he asked judgment, and sat down amidst great applause.

Mr. Wickham then rose, and made an argument of a similar pattern. No rule, he said, requires an impossibility. Mr. Marshall's quoit is twice as large as any other; and yet it flies from his arm like the iron ball at the Grecian games from the arm of Ajax. It is impossible for an ordinary quoit to move it. With much more of the same sort, he contended that it was a drawn game. After very animated voting, designed to keep up the uncertainty as long as possible, it was so decided. Another trial was had, and Marshall clearly won.[1]

Years later Chester Harding, who once painted Marshall, visited the Club. "I watched," says he, "for the coming of the old chief. He soon approached, with his coat on his arm and his hat in his hand, which he was using as a fan. He walked directly up to a large bowl of mint julep which had been prepared, and drank off a tumblerful, smacking his lips, and then turned to the company with a cheerful 'How are you, gentlemen?' He was looked upon as the best pitcher of the party and could throw heavier quoits than any other member of the club. The game began with great animation. There were several ties; and before long I saw the great Chief Justice of the United States

[1] J. B. Thayer, *John Marshall* (Riverside Biographical Series, 1904), pp. 134–36, paraphrasing G. W. Munford, *The Two Parsons* (Richmond, 1884), pp. 326–38.

down on his knees measuring the contested distance with a straw, with as much earnestness as if it had been a point of law; and if he proved to be in the right, the woods would ring with his triumphant shout." [1] What Wellesley remarked of the younger Pitt may be repeated of Marshall, that "unconscious of his superiority," he "plunged heedlessly into the mirth of the hour" and was endowed with "a gay heart and social spirit beyond any man of his time."

As a hero of anecdotes Marshall almost rivals Lincoln. Many of the tales preserved are doubtless apocryphal, but this qualification hardly lessens their value as contemporary impressions of his character and habits. They show for what sort of anecdotes his familiarly known personality had an affinity.

The Chief Justice's entire freedom from ostentation and the gentleness with which he could rebuke it in others is illustrated in a story often told. Going early to the market one morning he came upon a youth who was fuming and swearing because he could get no one to carry his turkey home for him. Marshall proffered his services. Arriving at the house the young man asked, "What shall I

[1] Thayer, *op. cit.*, pp. 132–33.

pay you?" "Oh, nothing," was the reply; "it was on my way, and no trouble." As Marshall walked away, the young man inquired of a bystander, "Who is that polite old man that brought home my turkey for me?" "That," was the answer, "is Judge Marshall, Chief Justice of the United States."

Of the same general character is an anecdote which has to do with a much earlier period when Marshall was still a practicing attorney. An old farmer who was involved in a lawsuit came to Richmond to attend its trial. "Who is the best lawyer in Richmond?" he asked of his host, the innkeeper of the Eagle tavern. The latter pointed to a tall, ungainly, bareheaded man who had just passed, eating cherries from his hat and exchanging jests with other loiterers like himself. "That is he," said the innkeeper; "John Marshall is his name." But the old countryman, who had a hundred dollars in his pocket, proposed to spend it on something more showy and employed a solemn, black-coated, and much powdered bigwig. The latter turned out in due course to be a splendid illustration of the proverb that "fine feathers do not make fine birds." This the crestfallen rustic soon discovered. Meantime he had listened with amazement and growing admiration to an argument by

Marshall in a cause which came on before his own. He now went up to Marshall and, explaining his difficulty, offered him the five dollars which the exactions of the first attorney still left him, and besought his aid. With a humorous remark about the power of a black coat and powdered wig Marshall good-naturedly accepted the retainer.

The religious bent of the Chief Justice's mind is illustrated in another story, which tells of his arriving toward the close of day at an inn in one of the counties of Virginia, and falling in with some young men who presently began ardently to debate the question of the truth or falsity of the Christian religion. From six until eleven o'clock the young theologians argued keenly and ably on both sides of the question. Finally one of the bolder spirits exclaimed that it was impossible to overcome prejudices of long standing and, turning to the silent visitor, asked: "Well, my old gentleman, what do you think of these things?" To their amazement the "old gentleman" replied for an hour in an eloquent and convincing defense of the Christian religion, in which he answered in order every objection the young men had uttered. So impressive was the simplicity and loftiness of his discourse that the erstwhile critics were completely silenced.

In truth, Marshall's was a reverent mind, and it sprang instinctively to the defense of ideas and institutions whose value had been tested. Unfortunately, in his *Life of Washington* Marshall seems to have given this propensity a somewhat undue scope. There were external difficulties in dealing with such a subject apart from those inherent in a great biography, and Marshall's volumes proved to be a general disappointment. Still hard pressed for funds wherewith to meet his Fairfax investment, he undertook this work shortly after he became Chief Justice, at the urgent solicitation of Judge Bushrod Washington, the literary executor of his famous uncle Marshall had hoped to make this incursion into the field of letters a very remunerative one, for he and Washington had counted on some thirty thousand subscribers for the work. The publishers however, succeeded in obtaining only about a quarter of that number, owing partly at least to the fact that Jefferson had no sooner learned of the enterprise than his jealous mind conceived the idea that the biography must be intended for partisan purposes. He accordingly gave the alarm to the Republican press and forbade the Federal postmasters to take orders for the book. At the same time he asked his friend Joel Barlow, then residing in Paris, to prepare a counterblast, for which he declared himself to be "rich in materials." The author of the *Columbiad*, however, declined this hazardous commission, possibly because he was unwilling to stand sponsor for the malicious recitals that afterwards saw light in the pages of the *Anas*.

But apart from this external opposition to the biography, Marshall found a source of even keener disappointment in the literary defects due to the haste with which he had done his work. The first three volumes had appeared in 1804, the fourth in 1805, and the fifth, which is much the best, in 1807. Republican critics dwelt with no light hand upon the deficiencies of these volumes, and Marshall himself sadly owned that the "inelegancies" in the first were astonishingly numerous. But the shortcomings of the work as a satisfactory biography are more notable than its lapses in diction. By a design apparently meant to rival the improvisations of *Tristram Shandy*, the birth of the hero is postponed for an entire volume, in which the author traces the settlement of the country. At the opening of the second volume "the birth of young Mr. Washington" is gravely announced, to be followed by an account of the Father of his Country so devoid of intimate touches that it might easily have

14

been written by one who had never seen George Washington.

Nevertheless, these pages of Marshall's do not lack acute historical judgments. He points out, for instance, that, if the Revolution had ended before the Articles of Confederation were adopted, permanent disunion might have ensued and that, faulty as it was, the Confederation "preserved the idea of Union until the good sense of the Nation adopted a more efficient system." Again, in his account of the events leading up to the Convention of 1787, Marshall rightly emphasizes facts which subsequent writers have generally passed by with hardly any mention, so that students may read this work with profit even today. But the chief importance of these volumes lay, after all, in the additional power which the author himself derived from the labor of their preparation. In so extensive an undertaking Marshall received valuable training for his later task of laying the foundations of Constitutional Law in America. One of his chief assets on the bench, as we have already seen, was his complete confidence in his own knowledge of the intentions of the Constitution — a confidence which was grounded in the consciousness that he had written the history of the Constitution's framing.

Most of Marshall's correspondence, which is not voluminous, deals with politics or legal matters. But there are letters in which the personal side of the Chief Justice is revealed. He gives his friend Story a touching account of the loss of two of his children. He praises old friends and laments his inability to make new ones. He commends Jane Austen, whose novels he has just finished reading. "Her flights," he remarks, "are not lofty, she does not soar on eagle's wings, but she is pleasing, interesting, equable, and yet amusing." He laments that he "can no longer debate and yet cannot apply his mind to anything else." One recalls Darwin's similar lament that his scientific work had deprived him of all liking for poetry.

The following letter, which Marshall wrote the year before his death to his grandson, a lad of fourteen or fifteen, is interesting for its views on a variety of subjects and is especially pleasing for its characteristic freedom from condescension:

I had yesterday the pleasure of receiving your letter of the 29th of November, and am quite pleased with the course of study you are pursuing. Proficiency in Greek and Latin is indispensable to an accomplished scholar, and may be of great real advantage in our progress through human life. Cicero deserves to be studied still more for his talents than for the improvement in language to be derived from reading him. He was unquestionably, with the single exception of Demosthenes, the greatest orator among the ancients. He was too a profound Philosopher. His "de officiis" is among the most valuable treatises I have ever seen in the Latin language.

History is among the most essential departments of knowledge; and, to an American, the histories of England and of the United States are most instructive. Every man ought to be intimately acquainted with the history of his own country. Those of England and of the United States are so closely connected that the former seems to be introductory to the latter. They form one whole. Hume, as far as he goes, to the revolution of 1688, is generally thought the best Historian of England. Others have continued his narrative to a late period, and it will be necessary to read them also.

There is no exercise of the mind from which more valuable improvement is to be drawn than from composition. In every situation of life the result of early practice will be valuable. Both in speaking and writing, the early habit of arranging our thoughts with regularity, so as to point them to the object to be proved, will be of great advantage. In both, clearness and precision are most essential qualities. The man who by seeking embellishment hazards confusion, is greatly mistaken in what constitutes good writing. The meaning ought never to be mistaken. Indeed the readers should never be obliged to search for it. The writer should always express himself so clearly as to make it impossible to misunderstand him. He should be comprehended without an effort.

The first step towards writing and speaking clearly is

to think clearly. Let the subject be perfectly understood, and a man will soon find words to convey his
meaning to others. Blair, whose lectures are greatly and
justly admired, advises a practice well worthy of being
observed. It is to take a page of some approved writer
and read it over repeatedly until the matter, not the
words, be fully impressed on the mind. Then write, in
your own language, the same matter. A comparison of
the one with the other will enable you to remark and
correct your own defects. This course may be pursued
after having made some progress in composition. In
the commencement, the student ought carefully to repe-
ruse what he has written, correct, in the first instance,
every error of orthography and grammar. A mistake
in either is unpardonable. Afterwards revise and improve the language.

I am pleased with both your pieces of composition.
The subjects are well chosen and of the deepest interest.
Happiness is pursued by all, though too many mistake
the road by which the greatest good is to be successfully followed. Its abode is not always in the palace or
the cottage. Its residence is the human heart, and its
inseparable companion is a quiet conscience. Of this,
Religion is the surest and safest foundation. The individual who turns his thoughts frequently to an om-
nipotent omniscient and all perfect being, who feels his
dependence on, and his infinite obligations to that being will avoid that course of life which must harrow up
the conscience.

Marshall was usually most scrupulous to steer
clear of partisan politics both in his letters and in

his conversation, so that on one occasion he was much aroused by a newspaper article which had represented him "as using language which could be uttered only by an angry party man." But on political issues of a broader nature he expressed himself freely in the strict privacy of correspondence at least, and sometimes identified himself with public movements, especially in his home State. For instance, he favored the gradual abolition of slavery by private emancipation rather than by governmental action. In 1823 he became first president of the Richmond branch of the Colonization Society; five years later he presided over a convention to promote internal improvements in Virginia; and in 1829 he took a prominent part in the deliberations of the State Constitutional Convention.

In the broader matters of national concern his political creed was in thorough agreement with his constitutional doctrine. Nullification he denounced as "wicked folly," and he warmly applauded Jackson's proclamation of warning to South Carolina. But Marshall regarded with dismay Jackson's aggrandizement of the executive branch, and the one adverse criticism he has left of the Constitution is of the method provided for the election of the President. In this connection he wrote in 1830: "My own private mind has been slowly and reluctantly advancing to the belief that the present mode of choosing the Chief Magistrate threatens the most serious danger to the public happiness. The passions of men are influenced to so fearful an extent, large masses are so embittered against each other, that I dread the consequences. . . . Age is, perhaps, unreasonably timid. Certain it is that I now dread consequences that I once thought imaginary. I feel disposed to take refuge under some less turbulent and less dangerous mode of choosing the Chief Magistrate." Then follows the suggestion that the people of the United States elect a body of persons equal in number to one-third of the Senate and that the President be chosen from among this body by lot. Marshall's suggestion seems absurd enough today, but it should be remembered that his fears of national disorder as a result of strong party feeling at the time of presidential elections were thoroughly realized in 1860 when Lincoln's election led to secession and civil war, and that sixteen years later, in the Hayes-Tilden contest, a second dangerous crisis was narrowly averted.

In the campaign of 1832 Marshall espoused privately the cause of Clay and the United States

Bank, and could not see why Virginia should not be of the same opinion. Writing to Story in the midst of the campaign he said: "We are up to the chin in politics. Virginia was always insane enough to be opposed to the Bank of the United States, and therefore hurrahs for the veto. But we are a little doubtful how it may work in Pennsylvania. It is not difficult to account for the part New York may take. She has sagacity enough to see her interests in putting down the present Bank. Her mercantile position gives her a control, a commanding control, over the currency and the exchanges of the country, if there be no Bank of the United States. Going for herself she may approve this policy; but Virginia ought not to drudge for her." To the end of his days Marshall seems to have refused to recognize that the South had a sectional interest to protect, or at least that Virginia's interests were sectional; her attachment to State Rights he assigned to the baneful influence of Jeffersonianism.

The year 1831 dealt Marshall two severe blows. In that year his robust constitution manifested the first signs of impairment, and he was forced to undergo an operation for stone. In the days before anæsthetics, such an operation, especially in the case of a person of his advanced years, was attended with great peril. He faced the ordeal with the utmost composure. His physician tells of visiting Marshall the morning he was to submit to the knife and of finding him at breakfast:

He received me with a pleasant smile . . . and said, "Well, Doctor, you find me taking breakfast, and I assure you I have had a good one. I thought it very probable that this might be my last chance, and therefore I was determined to enjoy it and eat heartily." . . . He said that he had not the slightest desire to live, laboring under the sufferings to which he was subjected, and that he was perfectly ready to take all the chances of an operation, and he knew there were many against him. . . . After he had finished his breakfast, I administered him some medicine; he then inquired at what hour the operation would be performed. I mentioned the hour of eleven. He said "Very well; do you wish me for any other purpose, or may I lie down and go to sleep?" I was a good deal surprised at this question, but told him that if he could sleep it would be very desirable. He immediately placed himself upon the bed and fell into a profound sleep, and continued so until I was obliged to rouse him in order to undergo the operation. He exhibited the same fortitude, scarcely uttering a murmur throughout the whole procedure which, from the nature of his complaint, was necessarily tedious.

The death of his wife on Christmas Day of the same year was a heavy blow. Despite her invalidism, she was a woman of much force of character and many graces of mind, to which Marshall rendered touching tribute in a quaint eulogy composed for one of his sons on the first anniversary of her death:

Her judgment was so sound and so safe that I have often relied upon it in situations of some perplexity. . . . Though serious as well as gentle in her deportment, she possessed a good deal of chaste, delicate, and playful wit, and if she permitted herself to indulge this talent, told her little story with grace, and could mimic very successfully the peculiarities of the person who was its subject. She had a fine taste for belle-lettre reading. . . . This quality, by improving her talents for conversation, contributed not inconsiderably to make her a most desirable and agreeable companion. It beguiled many of those winter evenings during which her protracted ill health and her feeble nervous system confined us entirely to each other. I shall never cease to look back on them with deep interest and regret. . . . She felt deeply the distress of others, and indulged the feeling liberally on objects she believed to be meritorious. . . . She was a firm believer in the faith inculcated by the Church in which she was bred, but her soft and gentle temper was incapable of adopting the gloomy and austere dogmas which some of its professors have sought to engraft on it.

Marshall believed women were the intellectual equals of men, because he was convinced that they possessed in a high degree "those qualities which make up the sum of human happiness and transform the domestic fireside into an elysium," and not because he thought they could compete on even terms in the usual activities of men.

Despite these "buffetings of fate," the Chief Justice was back in Washington in attendance upon Court in February, 1832, and daily walked several miles to and from the Capitol. In the following January his health appeared to be completely restored. "He seemed," says Story, with whom he messed, along with Justices Thompson and Duval, "to revive, and enjoy anew his green old age." This year Marshall had the gratification of receiving the tribute of Story's magnificent dedication of his *Commentaries* to him. With characteristic modesty, the aged Chief Justice expressed the fear that his admirer had "consulted a partial friendship farther than your deliberate judgment will approve." He was especially interested in the copy intended for the schools, but he felt that "south of the Potomac, where it is most wanted it will be least used," for, he continued, "it is a Mohammedan rule never to dispute with the ignorant, and we of the true faith in the South adjure the contamination of infidel political works. It would give our orthodox nullifyer a fever to read the heresies of your Commentaries. A whole school might be infected by the atmosphere of a single copy should it be placed on one of the shelves of a bookcase."

Marshall sat on the Bench for the last time in the January term of 1835. Miss Harriet Martineau, who was in Washington during that winter, has left a striking picture of the Chief Justice as he appeared in these last days. "How delighted," she writes, "we were to see Judge Story bring in the tall, majestic, bright-eyed old man, — old by chronology, by the lines on his composed face, and by his services to the republic; but so dignified, so fresh, so present to the time, that no compassionate consideration for age dared mix with the contemplation of him."

Marshall was, however, a very sick man, suffering constant pain from a badly diseased liver. The ailment was greatly aggravated, moreover, by "severe contusions" which he received while returning in the stage from Washington to Richmond. In June he went a second time to Philadelphia for medical assistance, but his case was soon seen to be hopeless He awaited death with his usual serenity, and two days before it came he composed the

modest epitaph which appeared upon his tomb:
JOHN MARSHALL, SON OF THOMAS AND MARY MAR-
SHALL, WAS BORN ON THE 24TH OF SEPTEMBER,
1755, INTERMARRIED WITH MARY WILLIS AMBLER
THE 3D OF JANUARY, 1783, DEPARTED THIS LIFE
THE — DAY OF —, 18 — . He died the evening of
July 6, 1835, surrounded by three of his sons. The
death of the fourth, from an accident while he was
hurrying to his father's bedside, had been kept
from him. He left also a daughter and numerous
grandchildren.

Marshall's will is dated April 9, 1832, and has
five codicils of subsequent dates attached. After
certain donations to grandsons named John and
Thomas, the estate, consisting chiefly of his portion
of the Fairfax purchase, was to be divided equally
among his five children. To the daughter and her
descendants were also secured one hundred shares
of stock which his wife had held in the Bank of the
United States, but in 1835 these were probably of
little value. His faithful body servant Robin was
to be emancipated and, if he chose, sent to Liberia,
in which event he should receive one hundred
dollars. But if he preferred to remain in the Commonwealth, he should receive but fifty dollars; and
if it turned out to "be impracticable to liberate

him consistently with law and his own inclination,"
he was to select his master from among the children, "that he may always be treated as a faithful
meritorious servant."

The Chief Justice's death evoked many eloquent
tributes to his public services and private excel-
lencies, but none more just and appreciative than
that of the officers of court and members of the bar
of his own circuit who knew him most intimately.
It reads as follows:

John Marshall, late Chief Justice of the United States,
having departed this life since the last Term of the
Federal Circuit Court for this district, the Bench, Bar,
and Officers of the Court, assembled at the present
Term, embrace the first opportunity to express their
profound and heartfelt respect for the memory of the
venerable judge, who presided in this Court for thirty-
five years — with such remarkable diligence in office,
that, until he was disabled by the disease which removed him from life, he was never known to be absent
from the bench, during term time, even for a day, —
with such indulgence to counsel and suitors, that every
body's convenience was consulted, but his own, — with
a dignity, sustained without effort, and, apparently,
without care to sustain it, to which all men were solicitous to pay due respect, — with such profound sagacity, such quick penetration, such acuteness, clearness,
strength, and comprehension of mind, that in his hand,
the most complicated causes were plain, the weightiest

and most difficult, easy and light, — with such striking
impartiality and justice, and a judgment so sure, as to
inspire universal confidence, so that few appeals were
ever taken from his decisions, during his long administration of justice in the Court, and those only in cases
where he himself expressed doubt, — with such modesty, that he seemed wholly unconscious of his own
gigantic powers, — with such equanimity, such benig-
nity of temper, such amenity of manners, that not only
none of the judges, who sat with him on the bench, but
no member of the bar, no officer of the court, no juror,
no witness, no suitor, in a single instance, ever found or
imagined, in any thing said or done, or omitted by him,
the slightest cause of offence.

His private life was worthy of the exalted character
he sustained in public station. The unaffected simplicity of his manners; the spotless purity of his morals;
his social, gentle, cheerful disposition; his habitual self-
denial, and boundless generosity towards others; the
strength and constancy of his attachments; his kindness
to his friends and neighbours; his exemplary conduct in
the relations of son, brother, husband, father; his numerous charities; his benevolence towards all men, and his
ever active beneficence; these amiable qualities shone so
conspicuously in him, throughout his life, that, highly
as he was respected, he had the rare happiness to be yet
more beloved.

There is no more engaging figure in American
history, none more entirely free from disfiguring
idiosyncrasy, than the son of Thomas Marshall.

CHAPTER IX

IN the brief period of twenty-seven months following the death of Marshall the Supreme Court received a new Chief Justice and five new Associate Justices. The effect of this change in personnel upon the doctrine of the Court soon became manifest. In the eleventh volume of Peters's *Reports*, the first issued while Roger B. Taney was Chief Justice, are three decisions of constitutional cases sustaining state laws which on earlier argument Marshall had assessed as unconstitutional. The first of these decisions gave what was designated "the complete, unqualified, and exclusive" power of the State to regulate its "internal police" the right of way over the "commerce clause"[1]; the second practically nullified the constitutional prohibition against "bills of credit" in deference to the same high prerogative[2]; the third curtailed

[1] Milton *vs*. New York, 11 Peters, 102.
[2] Briscoe *vs*. Bank of Kentucky, 11 Peters, 257.

the operation of the "obligation of contracts" clause as a protection of public grants.[1] Story, voicing "an earnest desire to vindicate his [Marshall's] memory from the imputation of rashness," filed passionate and unavailing dissents. With difficulty he was dissuaded from resigning from a tribunal whose days of influence he thought gone by.[2] During the same year Justice Henry Baldwin, another of Marshall's friends and associates, published his *View of the Constitution*, in which he rendered high praise to the departed Chief Justice's qualifications as expounder of the Constitution. "No commentator," he wrote, "ever followed the text more faithfully, or ever made a commentary more accordant with its strict intention and language. . . . He never brought into action the powers of his mighty mind to find some meaning in plain words . . . above the comprehension of ordinary minds. . . . He knew the framers of the Constitution, who were his compatriots," he was

[1] Charles River Bridge Company *vs.* Warren Bridge Company, 11 Peters, 420.

[2] He wrote Justice McLean, May 10, 1837: "There will not, I fear, even in our day, be any case in which a law of a State or of Congress will be declared unconstitutional; for the old constitutional doctrines are fast fading away." *Life and Letters of Joseph Story*, vol. II, p. 272; see also p. 270, for Chancellor Kent's unfavorable reaction to these decisions.

himself the historian of its framing, wherefore, as its expositor, "he knew its objects, its intentions." Yet in the face of these admissions, Baldwin rejects Marshall's theory of the origin of the Constitution and the corollary doctrine of liberal construction. "The history and spirit of the times," he wrote, "admonish us that new versions of the Constitution will be promulgated to meet the varying course of political events or aspirations of power."

But the radical impulse soon spent itself. Chief Justice Taney himself was a good deal of a conservative. While he regarded the Supreme Court rather as an umpire between two sovereignties than as an organ of the National Government for the vigorous assertion of its powers, which was Marshall's point of view, Taney was not at all disposed to disturb the law as it had been declared by his predecessor in binding decisions. Then, too, the development of railroading and the beginning of immigration from Europe on a large scale reawakened the interest of a great part of the nation in keeping intercourse between the States untrammeled by local selfishness; and in 1851 the Court, heeding the spirit of compromise of the day, decisively accepted for the most important category of cases Marshall's principle of the exclusive control of interstate and foreign commerce by Congress.[1]

Still, until the eve of the Civil War, the theory of the Constitution held by the great body of the people, North as well as South, was that it was a compact of States. Then in December, 1860, South Carolina announced her secession from the Union. Buchanan's message of the same month performed the twofold service of refuting secession on State Rights principles and of demonstrating, albeit unwittingly, how impossible it was practically to combat the movement on the same principles. Lincoln brought the North back to Marshall's position when he remarked in his Inaugural Address: "Continue to execute all the express provisions of our National Constitution, and the Union will endure forever."

The Civil War has been characterized as "an appeal from the judgments of Marshall to the arbitrament of war." Its outcome restored the concept of the National Government as a territorial sovereign, present within the States by the superior mandate of the American People, and entitled to "execute on every foot of American soil the powers and functions that belong to

[1] Cooley *vs*. the Board of Wardens, 12 Howard, 299.

it."[1] These powers and functions are, moreover, today undergoing constant enlargement. No one now doubts that in any clash between national and state power it is national power which is entitled to be defined first, and few persons question that it ought to be defined in the light of Marshall's principle, that a Constitution designed for ages to come must be "adapted to the various crises of human affairs."

It is only when we turn to that branch of Constitutional Law which defines governmental power in relation to private rights that we lose touch with Marshall's principles. As we have seen, he dealt in absolutes: either power was given to an unlimited extent or it was withheld altogether. Today, however, the dominant rule in this field of Constitutional Law is the "rule of reason." In the last analysis, there are few private rights which are not subordinate to the general welfare; but, on the other hand, legislation which affects private rights must have a reasonable tendency to promote the general welfare and must not arbitrarily invade the rights of particular persons or classes. Inasmuch as the hard and fast rules of an age when conditions of life were simpler are no longer practicable under

[1] Justice Bradley in *ex parte* Siebold, 100 U. S., 371.

the more complex relationships of modern times, there is today an inevitable tendency to force these rules to greater flexibility.[1]

And this difference in the point of view of the judiciary connotes a general difference of outlook which makes itself felt today even in that field where Marshall wrought most enduringly. The Constitution was established under the sway of the idea of the balance of power, and with the purpose of effecting a compromise among a variety of more or less antagonistic interests, some of which were identified with the cause of local autonomy, others of which coalesced with the cause of National Supremacy. The Nation and the States were regarded as competitive forces, and a condition of tension between them was thought to be not only normal but desirable. The modern point of view is very different. Local differences have to a great extent disappeared, and that general interest which

---

[1] Notwithstanding what is said above, it is also true that the modern doctrine of "the police power" owes something to Marshall's interpretation of the "necessary and proper" clause in M'Culloch *vs.* Maryland, which is frequently offered nowadays as stating the authoritative definition of "a fair legislative discretion" in relation to private rights. Indeed this ingenious transposition was first suggested in Marshall's day. See Cowen (N. Y.), 585. But it never received his sanction and does not represent his point of view.

is the same for all the States is an ever deepening one. The idea of the competition of the States with the Nation is yielding to that of their coöperation in public service. And it is much the same with the relation of the three departments of Government. The notion that they have antagonistic interests to guard is giving way to the perception of a general interest guarded by all according to their several faculties. In brief, whereas it was the original effort of the Constitution to preserve a somewhat complex set of values by nice differentiations of power, the present tendency, born of a surer vision of a single national welfare, is toward the participation of all powers in a joint effort for a common end.

But though Marshall's work has been superseded at many points, there is no fame among American statesmen more strongly bulwarked by great and still vital institutions. Marshall established judicial review; he imparted to an ancient legal tradition a new significance; he made his Court one of the great political forces of the country; he founded American Constitutional Law; he formulated, more tellingly than any one else and for a people whose thought was permeated with legalism, the principles on which the integrity and ordered growth

of their Nation have depended.   Springing from
the twin rootage of Magna Charta and the Declaration of Independence, his judicial statesman-
ship finds no parallel in the salient features of its
achievement outside our own annals.

BIBLIOGRAPHICAL NOTE

ALL accounts of Marshall's career previous to his appointment as Chief Justice have been superseded by Albert J. Beveridge's two admirable volumes, *The Life of John Marshall* (Boston, 1916). The author paints on a large canvas and with notable skill. His work is history as well as biography. His ample plan enables him to quote liberally from Marshall's writings and from all the really valuable first-hand sources. Both text and notes are valuable repositories of material. Beveridge has substantially completed a third volume covering the first decade of Marshall's chief-justiceship, and the entire work will probably run to five volumes.

Briefer accounts of Marshall covering his entire career will be found in Henry Flanders's *Lives and Times of the Chief Justices of the Supreme Court* (1875) and Van Santvoord's *Sketches of the Lives, Times, and Judicial Services of the Chief Justices of the Supreme Court* (1882). Two excellent brief sketches are J. B. Thayer's *John Marshall* (1901) in the *Riverside Biographical Series*, and W. D. Lewis's essay in the second volume of *The Great American Lawyers*, 8 vols. (Philadelphia, 1907), of which he is also the editor. The latter is particularly happy in its blend of the personal and legal, the biographical and critical. A. B. Magruder's *John Marshall* (1898) in the *American Statesman Series* ll considerably below the general standard maintained by that excellent series.

The centennial anniversary of Marshall's accession to the Supreme Bench was generally observed by Bench and Bar throughout the United States, and many of the addresses on the great Chief Justice's life and judicial services delivered by distinguished judges and lawyers on that occasion were later collected by John F. Dillon and published in *John Marshall, Life, Character, and Judicial Services*, 3 vols. (Chicago, 1903). In volume XIII of the *Green Bag* will be found a skillfully constructed mosaic biography of Marshall drawn from these addresses.

The most considerable group of Marshall's letters yet published are those to Justice Story, which will be found in the *Massachusetts Historical Society Proceedings*, Second Series, volume XIV, pp. 321–60. These and most of the Chief Justice's other letters which have thus far seen the light of day will be found in J. E. Oster's *Political and Economic Doctrines of John Marshall* (New York, 1914). Here also will be found a copy of Marshall's will, of the autobiography which he prepared in 1818 for Delaplaine's *Repository* but which was never published there, and of his eulogy of his wife. The two principal sources of Marshall's anecdotes are the *Southern Literary Messenger*, volume II, p. 181 ff., and Henry Howe's *Historical Collections of Virginia* (Charleston, 1845). Approaching the value of sources are Joseph Story's *Discourse upon the Life, Character, and Services of the Hon. John Marshall* (1835) and Horace Binney's *Eulogy* (1835), both of which were pronounced by personal friends shortly after Marshall's death and both of which are now available in volume III of Dillon's

compilation, cited above. The value of Ma.
of Washington as bearing on the origin of his o.
of view in politics was noted in the text (Chapter

Marshall's great constitutional decisions are, of cou.
accessible in the *Reports*, but they have also been a.
sembled into a single volume by John M. Dillon, *John
Marshall; Complete Constitutional Decisions* (Chicago,
1903), and into two instructively edited volumes by
Joseph P. Cotton, *Constitutional Decisions of John Marshall* (New York, 1905). Story's famous *Commentaries
on the Constitution* gives a systematic presentation
of Marshall's constitutional doctrines, which is fortified
at all points by historical reference; the second edition
is the best. For other contemporary evaluations of
Marshall's decisions, often hostile, see early volumes
of the *North American Review* and Niles's *Register;* also
the volumes of the famous John Taylor of Caroline. A
brief general account of later date of the decisions is to
be found in the *Constitutional History of the United
States as Seen in the Development of American Law* (New
York, 1889), a course of lectures before the Political
Science Association of the University of Michigan. De-
tailed commentary of a high order of scholarship is
furnished by Walter Malins Rose's *Notes* to the Lawyers' Edition of the *United States Reports*, 13 vols.
(1899–1901). The more valuable of Marshall's decisions on circuit are collected in J. W. Brockenbrough's
two volumes of *Reports of Cases Decided by the Hon. John
Marshall* (Philadelphia, 1837), and his rulings at Burr's
Trial are to be found in Robertson's *Reports of the Trials
of Colonel Aaron Burr*, 2 vols. (1808).

Marshall's associates on the Supreme Bench are
pleasingly sketched in Hampton L. Carson's *Supreme*

Court of the United States (Philadelphia, 1891), which also gives many interesting facts bearing on the history of the Court itself. In the same connection Charles Warren's *History of the American Bar* (Boston, 1911) is also valuable both for the facts which it records and for the guidance it affords to further material. Of biographies of contemporaries and coworkers of Marshall, the most valuable are John P. Kennedy's *Memoirs of the Life of William Wirt,* 2 vols. (Philadelphia, 1860); William Wetmore Story's *Life and Letters of Joseph Story,* 2 vols. (Boston, 1851); and William Kent's *Memoirs and Letters of James Kent* (Boston, 1898). Everett P. Wheeler's *Daniel Webster the Expounder of the Constitution* (1905) is instructive, but claims far too much for Webster's influence upon Marshall's views. New England has never yet quite forgiven Virginia for having had the temerity to take the formative hand in shaping our Constitutional Law. The vast amount of material brought together in Gustavus Myers's *History of the Supreme Court* (Chicago, 1912) is based on purely *ex parte* statements and is so poorly authenticated as to be valueless. He writes from the socialistic point of view and fluctuates between the desire to establish the dogma of "class bias" by a coldly impartial examination of the "facts" and the desire to start a scandal reflecting on individual reputations.

The literature of eulogy and appreciation is, for all practical purposes, exhausted in Dillon's collection. But a reference should be made here to a brief but pertinent and excellently phrased comment on the great Chief Justice in Woodrow Wilson's *Constitutional Government in the United States* (New York, 1908), pp. 158–9.

INDEX

Adams, John, and "midnight judges," 22–23; appoints Marshall Chief Justice, 23–24, 51; Marshall defends, 48

Adams, J. Q., *Memoirs*, cited, 71 (note); record of Giles's views on impeachment, 74–75; on Randolph, 81–82; quoted, 126

Addison, Alexander, 59

Alien and Sedition laws, 47; *see also* Sedition Act

Ambler, Mary, Marshall marries, 30; death, 217–18

Articles of Confederation, 3–4

Baldwin, Henry, *View of the Constitution*, praise of Marshall, 225–26

Bank, U. S., 124–26; Marshall and, 214–15; *see also* M'Culloch *vs.* Maryland

Barbecue Club, 202–04

Barlow, Joel, 208–09

Barron *vs.* Baltimore, 191

Bartlett, attorney in Dartmouth College case, 159, 163

Benton, T. H., *Abridgment of the Debates of Congress*, cited, 66 (note)

Beveridge, A. J., *The Life of John Marshall*, quoted, 31, 43, 201

Blair, Rev., and anecdote of Barbecue Club, 203–04

Blair, Justice John, of Virginia, 15, 19

Blennerhassett, Harman, and Burr, 87, 89, 105; describes Eaton, 92

Blennerhassett's Island, 87, 103

Bollmann, Erick, witness at Burr's trial, 92–93, 94, 108, 109

Botts, Benjamin, defends Burr, 92

Bradley, Justice J. P., cited, 144 (note); quoted, 227–28

Breckinridge, John, of Kentucky, 61, 62

Briscoe *vs.* Bank of Kentucky, 191

Brown, Francis, President of Dartmouth College, 164

Brown *vs.* Maryland, 142–44, 171, 190

Buchanan, James, and secession, 227

Burr, Aaron, and Marshall, 50; Vice-President, 76; favors to, 82–83; "conspiracy" and trial, 86 *et seq.*

Calder *vs.* Bull, 150, 154

Calhoun, J. C., and state sovereignty, 192

Callender, J. T., tried for sedition, 57, 73, 79

Campbell, clergyman, teaches John Marshall, 28

Campbell, lawyer of Richmond, 32, 78

Charles River Bridge Company *vs.* Warren Bridge Company, 225 (note)

Chase, Justice Samuel, of Maryland, 19, 57, 71–72, 150; impeachment, 72, 73–83, 112–13

237

Cherokee Nation vs. Georgia, 193
Chisholm vs. Georgia, 18
Cincinnati, Burr goes to, 87
Civil War, 226
Clay, Henry, Marshall and, 214
Clinton, De Witt, Governor of New York, 164
Cohens vs. Virginia, 179
Commerce, Marshall's opinion of congressional control of, 139–42; see also Congress
Congress, and Supreme Court, 7, 12–13; impeachments, 71–83; control of commerce, 139–143, 145, 171, 226
Connecticut, statute excluding Fulton-Livingston vessels, 136
Constitution, relation of Supreme Court to, 7–13; principles from Marshall's interpretation of, 144–45
Constitutional Convention and state coercion, 4–5
Contracts, sanctity of, 147 et seq.
Cooley vs. the Board of Wardens, 227
Cooper, Thomas, tried for sedition, 57
Corn Tassel, Cherokee Indian, 193
Craig vs. Missouri, 192–93
Cumberland Road Bill vetoed, 188
Cushing, Justice William, of Massachusetts, 15, 17, 116
Cushing, Mrs., wife of Justice, 17

Dartmouth College vs. Woodward, 124, 154 et seq.
Dickinson, John, of Delaware, on removal of judges, 6; Jefferson writes to, 23; President of Pennsylvania, 59 (note)
Dodd, W. E., Chief Justice Marshall and Virginia, cited, 174 (note)
Duval, Justice Gabriel, 219; and Dartmouth College case, 163

Eaton, William, witness at Burr's trial, 92, 101
Elliot, J., Debates, 36, 38
Ellsworth, Oliver, 76; on state coercion, 5; author of Judiciary Act (1789), 14; Chief Justice, 20; resigns, 23, 175
Emmet, T. A., lawyer of New York, 136
Enquirer, Richmond, 183
Espionage Act of June 15, 1917, 110
Evans, Charles, Report, cited, 71 (note)

Federalist, 5, 13, 15, 18, 124, 175
Fletcher vs. Peck, 151–54, 159, 166
Fries, John, tried for treason, 57, 73, 79
Fries's Rebellion, 21
Fulton, Robert, steamboat grant to, 135

Gallatin, Albert, 48, 82
Georgia, land grant case, 151–54; controversy with Supreme Court, 193–94
Gerry, Elbridge, 45
Gibbons vs. Ogden, 130, 135–42, 145, 171, 189
Giles, W. B., of Virginia, 62, 74–75, 78, 82
Goodrich, C. A., Professor of Yale, 162 (note)
Green vs. Biddle, 184, 188
Griffin, Judge, at Burr's trial, 95

Hamilton, Alexander, 13, 36, 45, 50, 86, 121, 122; and U. S. Bank, 124–26
Harding, Chester, quoted, 204–205
Hay, George, and Sedition Act, 79; U. S. District Attorney, 91, 98, 113–14
Hayes, Samuel (or Haze), 155–56
Heath testifies against Chase, 79

Henry, Patrick, at Virginia Convention, 37, 38; supports Marshall, 48

Holmes, John, and Dartmouth College case, 163

Holmes, Justice O. W., on Marshall, 121

Hopkinson, Joseph, defends Chase, 80; in Bank case, 128; and Dartmouth College case, 162

Hunter *vs.* Martin, 174–77, 179

Impeachments, Pickering, 71–73; Chase, 73–83; of Pennsylvania State Supreme Court judges, 84

Indians, and Dartmouth College, 155, 158; and Georgia, 193

Iredell, Justice James, of North Carolina, 15

Jackson, Andrew, and Burr, 92; President, 191; and controversy between Supreme Court and Georgia, 194

Jay, John, of New York, Chief Justice, 15–16, 19–20, 196

Jefferson, Thomas, 25, 28, 166; elected President, 22; and the Judiciary, 23, 53, *et seq.*, 182–183; Governor of Virginia, 30; and Marshall, 46, 50, 55, 94–95, 96, 97–98, 108, 120; inauguration, 55–56; Marbury *vs.* Madison, 64–66; and Martin, 77, 78; and Burr, 82, 88–89, 90, 111, 113; and Johnson, 115; and U. S. Bank, 125; on Dartmouth College question, 157; criticism of Marshall's *Life of Washington*, 208–09

Johnson, Allen, *Jefferson and his Colleagues*, cited, 87 (note)

Johnson, R. M., of Kentucky, 185

Johnson, Justice William, 115, 151, 164

Jones, Walter, in Bank case, 128

Judiciary, establishment, 1 *et seq.*; removal of judges, 6; Jefferson's war on, 53 *et seq.*

Judiciary Act (1789), 14–16, 39, 192–93; Act (1801), 22, 60–63, 71

Kent, Chancellor James, of New York, 137, 138, 164, 225 (note)

Kentucky, anti-judicial movement, 58, 184–86, 187, 188

Kentucky Resolutions, 22, 127, 177

King, Rufus, on John Marshall, 44

Law Journal, Hall's, 183

Lee, R. E., 25

Lewis, attorney for Fries, 79

Lincoln, Abraham, and nationalism, 226

Livingston, Justice Brockholst, 164

Livingston, R. R., steamboat grant to, 135

Livingston family of New York, 16

Livingston *vs.* Van Ingen, 137 (note)

Lodge, H. C., on Marshall, 121

M'Culloch *vs.* Maryland, 124–135, 143, 182, 184, 190

McLean, Justice John, letter of Story to, quoted, 225 (note)

Madison, James, 82; on state coercion, 5; on state courts as national tribunals, 7; in Virginia Legislature, 34; Virginia Convention, 36, 37; and U. S. Bank, 126; *Journal*, cited, 175

Marbury *vs.* Madison, 64–71

Marsh, Charles, 164

Marshall, John, 18, 20, 22; and American constitutionalism, 2–3; appointed Chief Justice, 24, 51; born (1755), 25; early life, 25 *et seq.*; education, 27–28, 30; and the Revolution,

Marshall, John—*Continued*
29–30; marriage (1783), 30; practices law at Richmond, 31–32; in Virginia Legislature, 33; and adoption of Constitution, 35–38; Wirt's description of, 39–42; personal characteristics, 42; Federalist leader in Virginia, 43; and Jay Treaty, 43–44, 48; purchases Fairfax estate, 44–45; "X.Y.Z." mission, 45–46, 49; elected to Congress, 46–48; and Jefferson, 46, 50, 55, 94–95, 96, 97–98, 108, 120; in Washington, 53–54; first constitutional case, 64–71; and trial of Burr, 93 *et seq.*; and nationalism, 121 *et seq.*, 147; interpretation of Constitution, 144–45; and sanctity of contracts, 147 *et seq.*; and State Rights, 173 *et seq.*; as private citizen, 198 *et seq.*; as hero of anecdote, 205–06; religious bent, 206; *Life of Washington*, 34 (note), 208–10; correspondence, 211–213; and politics, 213–14; on method of electing President, 214–15; and U. S. Bank, 215–216; illness, 216–17; death of wife, 217–18; last years, 219–220; composes epitaph, 221; death, 221; will, 221–22; tribute, 221–22; Baldwin on, 925–26; bibliography, 233–36
Marshall, Thomas, father of John Marshall, 25, 27
Martin, Luther, of Maryland, on authority of federal legislation, 9; defends Chase, 76–77; 80–81; defends Burr, 92, 96; in Bank case, 128
Martin *vs.* Hunter's Lessee, 177–182
Martineau, Harriet, describes Marshall, 220
Maryland, attitude toward Judi-

ciary, 58; and U. S. Bank, *see* M'Culloch *vs.* Maryland
Mason, George, 38
Mason, Jeremiah, 158, 162
Mexico, "Burr's Conspiracy" against, 99
Morgan, General, witness at Burr's trial, 102
Morris, Gouverneur, quoted, 61
Morris, Robert, and Marshall, 45
Munford, G. W., *The Two Parsons*, cited, 204 (note)
Murch, Rachel, 155

Nashville (Tenn.), Burr goes to, 87
Natchez, Burr goes to, 87, 89
Nationalism, 121 *et seq.*, 227
Nereide, case of the, 118 (note)
New Jersey, statute excluding Fulton-Livingston vessels, 136
New Orleans, Wilkinson at, 89, 91; and Burr, 99
New York, and "Steamboat case," 136–42
New York City, Supreme Court in, 16
Newcastle (Del.), Chase at, 73
Nicholas, W. C., at Virginia Convention, 37
Nicholson, Joseph, and impeachment, 78; recall for Senators, 84
Nullification, 194; Marshall and, 214

Oakley, T. J., counsel for Ogden, 136
Ogden *vs.* Saunders, 190
Ohio, anti-judicial movement in, 184
Osborn *vs.* United States Bank, 189–90

Parton, James, *Life and Times of Aaron Burr*, quoted, 99–100
Passmore, Thomas, punished for contempt of court, 60

Pendleton, Edmund, lawyer of Richmond, 32

Pennsylvania, attitude toward Judiciary, 58, 84; protests Marshall's decision, 119

Philadelphia, Supreme Court at, 16; impeachment of judges at, 84; Burr goes to, 87

Pickering, Judge, of New Hampshire, impeachment, 71, 72-73

Pinckney, C. C., on "X.Y.Z." mission, 45

Pinkney, William, of Maryland, greatest lawyer of his day, 117-18; in Bank case, 128-129; in Dartmouth College case, 165

Plumer, William, Governor of New Hampshire, 156-58

Providence Bank vs. Billings, 191

Raleigh (N. C.), Marshall holds court at, 199

Randolph, Edmund, 25; defends Burr, 92

Randolph, John, 25, 32, 37, 54, 62, 90, 124; on Judiciary, 23; on Marshall, 52; and impeachment of Chase, 75, 78, 81-82; proposes amendment to Constitution, 83-84; at Burr's trial, 95

Reed, T. B., 169

Revolution, Marshall and, 29-30

Richardson, Chief Justice, 159

Richmond (Va.), Marshall practices law at, 31; Burr's trial at, 86 et seq.; Marshall holds court at, 199

Roane, Spencer, of Virginia, 174-78, 183

Robertson, Reports, cited, 109 (note)

Robins, Jonathan, British fugitive from justice, 48

Rodney, C. A., 78, 84

Rowan, Senator, of Kentucky, 187

Rutledge, John, of South Carolina, on state courts as national tribunals, 6-7; associate justice, 15

St. Louis, Burr goes to, 87

Satterlee vs. Matthewson, 191

Schooner Exchange vs. McFaddon et al, 118 (note)

Sedgwick, Theodore, on Marshall, 49-51

Sedition Act (1798), 21, 49, 57

Shays's Rebellion (1786), 34

"Shockoe Hill," Marshall's home at Richmond, 201

"Sidney, Algernon," pseudonym of Roane, 183

Smith, Jeremiah, 158-59, 163

South Carolina, nullification, 194; Jackson's proclamation to, 214; secession, 227

Spain, "Burr's Conspiracy" against, 89

State Rights, 7, 173, et seq.

"Steamboat case," see Gibbons vs. Ogden

Story, Justice Joseph, 109, 118, 220; Discourse, cited, 34 (note); and Marshall, 116, 150-51 (note), 183, 194, 195, 211, 216, 219, 225; quoted, 129, 201; Dartmouth College case, 163, 166; answer to Roane, 177-79

Sturges vs. Crowinshield, 124, 184, 190

Sullivan, attorney in Dartmouth College case, 159, 163

Supreme Court, relation to Constitution, 7-13; powers, 11; establishment, 12-13, 14; original bench, 15; in New York City, 16; in Philadelphia, 16; pioneer work, 17-19; need of leadership, 19-20; Act of Feb. 13, 1801, 22, 60-63, 71; in Washington, 54; defended by Virginia Assembly, 119-120; bill for enlargement, 186-187; controversy with Geor-

Supreme Court—*Continued*
gia, 193–94; number of cases
during Marshall's term of
office, 198; changes on bench,
223

Swartwout, Samuel, 93, 94, 108,
109

Taney, R. B., Chief Justice, 118,
224, 226
Taylor, John, of Caroline, 60, 192
Thayer, J. B., *John Marshall*,
quoted, 202–04
Thompson, Justice Smith, 219
Ticknor, George, describes Pink-
ney, 117–18
Tocqueville, Alexis de, opinion
of Supreme Court, 196–97
Todd, Justice Thomas, 163
Transportation, 188–89
Truxton, Commodore Thomas,
92, 102

United States *vs.* Peters, 118

Vincennes, Burr goes to, 87
Virginia, plan before Constitutional Convention, 8; Convention, 35–38; defends Supreme Court, 119–20; and U. S.
Bank, 216
Virginia Resolutions, 22, 127,
176, 177

Wakefield (Ala.), Burr captured
at, 90
Ware *vs.* Hylton, 44
Warren, Charles, cited, 185
(note)
Washington, Justice Bushrod,
115, 161, 163, 166, 190, 208

Washington, George, Marshall
and, 26–27, 34, 46; Marshall's
Life of, 34 (note), 208–10
Washington (D. C.), 53; Capitol,
54; Burr goes to, 87
Watson *vs.* Mercer, 191
Webster, Daniel, 29; and Bank
case, 128; Gibbons *vs.* Ogden,
136; Dartmouth College case,
159, 160–61, 163
Wentworth, John, Governor of
New Hampshire, 155
Wheelock, Rev. Eleazar, of
Connecticut, 155
Wheelock, Dr. John, son of Elea-
zar Wheelock, 156
Whisky Rebellion (1794), 21
Wickham, John, of Richmond,
32, 92, 202, 203–04
Wilkinson, James, 113; Mar-
shall's letter to, 35; military
commandant in Louisiana
Territory, 82; and Burr, 88,
93, 95; at New Orleans, 89,
91
William and Mary College, 30
Wilson, Justice James, of Penn-
sylvania, 15, 36
Wilson *vs.* Blackbird Creek
Marsh Company, 191
Wirt, William, *Letters of the
British Spy*, quoted, 39–42;
at Burr's trial, 91, 96–97, 102,
104–05, 110; Bank case, 128;
Gibbons *vs.* Ogden, 135–36;
Dartmouth College case, 163
Woodward, W. H., 158
Worcester *vs.* Georgia, 193–94
Wythe, George, 30, 32

"X.Y.Z." mission, 45–46